왕초보 영어 낭독 훈련

왕초보 영어 낭독 훈련

지은이 영어콘텐츠연구소
펴낸이 임상진
펴낸곳 (주)넥서스

초판 1쇄 인쇄 2017년 7월 10일
초판 1쇄 발행 2017년 7월 20일

출판신고 1992년 4월 3일 제311-2002-2호
10880 경기도 파주시 지목로 5
Tel (02)330-5500 Fax (02)330-5555

ISBN 979-11-6165-067-8 13740

출판사의 허락 없이 내용의 일부를
인용하거나 발췌하는 것을 금합니다.

가격은 뒤표지에 있습니다.
잘못 만들어진 책은 구입처에서 바꾸어 드립니다.

본 책은 『미국학교식 리딩 훈련북』(2012)의
개정판입니다.

www.nexusbook.com

ME-TIME BOOK
English

왕초보 영어 낭독 훈련

영어콘텐츠연구소 지음

넥서스

Preface

This book focuses on how to be a great reader when reading English texts and passages. Many Koreans might feel stress when they don't how to read an English passage correctly. There are many aspects that are important when reading an English passage. This book will help you to understand those areas, and it will provide you with useful tips on how to read English texts perfectly! The main segments which will be very practical and helpful are Step 2 and '영어발음을 향상시키는 방법'. Step 2 concentrates on intonation, cutting the lines, prolonged sounds and emphasizing certain words. You can listen to the passages that I read for you, and you can follow and practice along with me! I will point out how to do these steps and explain why certain things are very important when reading. If you follow these tips, you will be able to read more naturally and smoothly when you read many kinds of readings.

'영어발음을 향상시키는 방법' is also a very helpful part of this book. This part will teach you about the most common mistakes to avoid when reading or pronouncing certain words. It will give you some guidelines to follow when you read or pronounce certain words. In addition, there are some tongue twisters which will enable you to develop your pronunciation.

- Lynda Behk

이 책은 영어 Text나 Passage를 읽을 때 어떻게 하면 좋은 독자가 되는지 알려줍니다. 많은 한국분들이 영어 text를 제대로 읽지 못하면, 스트레스를 느끼게 됩니다. 영어를 읽을 때 중요하게 기억해야 할 부분들이 몇 가지 있습니다. 이 책은 그러한 부분들을 이해하는 데에 큰 도움이 될 것입니다. 또한 유용한 Tips들은 어떻게 영어 Text들을 제대로 읽을 수 있는지도 알려줄 것입니다. 특히, Step 2와 '영어발음을 향상시키는 방법'에서는 필수적인 노하우를 알려드릴 것입니다. Step 2는 억양과 끊어 읽기, 연음과 강조어를 다루고 있는데 제가 읽어 주는 Passages들을 같이 듣고 따라 읽으면서 연습하실 수 있습니다. 제가 어떻게 읽는지 그리고 어떤 부분을 강하게 읽어야 하는지에 대해서도 설명해 드릴 것입니다. 이런 Tips를 따라 읽으면, 다양한 영어 Passages를 자연스럽게 잘 읽을 수 있을 것입니다.

'영어발음을 향상시키는 방법'도 이 책에서 도움이 많이 되는 부분입니다. 읽을 때나 단어들을 발음할 때 가장 틀리기 쉬운 실수들을 어떻게 피할 수 있고, 어떻게 주의를 기울여야 하는지를 알려드립니다. 또한 발음에 주의를 해야 하는 단어의 발음 교정에 대해서도 언급하고 있습니다. Tongue Twisters에 관한 내용도 있어서, 발음 연습을 더 효과적으로 할 수 있습니다.

– 강의 및 감수 린다 백

린다 선생님이 언급한 Part 2와 '영어발음을 향상시키는 방법'은 이 책에서 가장 효과적인 부분입니다. 이외에도 이 책에서 제시하고 있는 5단계 낭독 훈련법을 따라 하시면 여러분의 Reading Skills와 Speaking Skills 향상에 큰 도움이 될 것입니다.

– 영어콘텐츠연구소

5단계 추천 낭독법

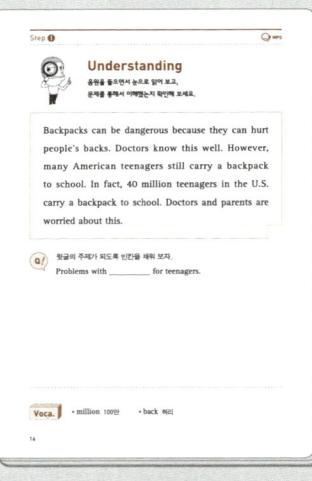

1단계
Understanding
지문 이해하기

낭독을 하기 전 Warm-up 단계로 독해 실력도 함께 향상시킨다.

 **MP3** 원어민 MP3 활용

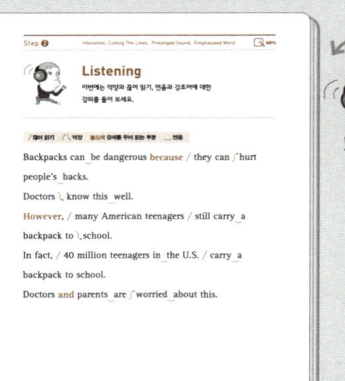

2단계
Listening
제대로 듣기

이 도서의 핵심이 되는 부분으로 억양과 끊어 읽기, 연음과 강조어에 대한 린다 선생님의 강의도 듣고, 실제 네이티브의 음성으로 제대로 들어 본다.

 **MP3** 강의 MP3 활용

3단계
Read Slowly
천천히 큰 소리로 읽기

린다 선생님 강의에서 천천히 읽는 부분을 따라 읽으면서 실제로 도서에 억양과 끊어 읽기, 연음과 강조어를 표시해 본다.

MP3 강의 MP3 활용

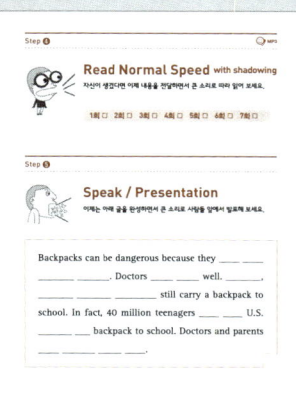

4단계
Read Normal Speed
말하듯 읽기

이제 본격적으로 따라 읽어 보는 시간이다. 듣고 따라 읽어 보고, 또 원어민 음성과 같이 Shadowing하면서 읽어 본다.

MP3 원어민 MP3 활용

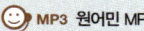

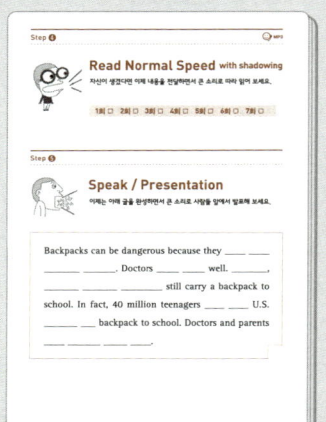

5단계
Speak / Presentation
발표하기

마지막 단계로 '말하기'에 도전하는 단계이다. 충분히 학습된 지문을 직접 자기의 이야기로 스피치에 도전해 본다.

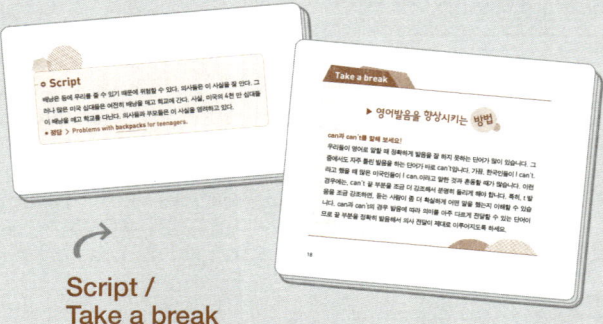

Script / Take a break
영어발음을 향상시키는 방법

미국 초등학교 린다 선생님의 "영어발음을 향상시키는 방법"을 전수받는다.
Level 3에서는 Tongue Twister를 통해서 영어발음을 연습해 본다.

Contents

Topic_01	**Wearing Backpacks Could Be Harmful** 배낭을 메고 다니는 것은 위험할 수 있다	15
Topic_02	**Harry Potter Is Truly Popular** 해리포터는 인기 절정	21
Topic_03	**The Junior High School Education System In Canada** 캐나다의 중등 교육 제도	27
Topic_04	**Let's Dance And Study** 공부도 하고 춤도 추자	33
Topic_05	**Save The Leatherback Sea Turtle!** 바다 장수거북이를 살리자!	39
Topic_06	**Hot Dogs For Americans** 미국인과 핫도그	45
Topic_07	**Read "Peanuts" And Laugh!** 만화 "피너츠"를 보고 웃어 보자!	51
Topic_08	**Cars Are Valuable Everywhere** 자동차는 어디에서나 중요하다	57
Topic_09	**Babies Prefer Beautiful People** 아기들은 아름다운 사람들을 좋아한다	63
Topic_10	**From Comic Books To The Screen** 만화책이 영화가 되다	69
Topic_11	**Join The Girl Scouts Now!** 지금, 걸 스카우트에 참여하자!	75
Topic_12	**Middle School Entrance Exam Changes** 중학교 입학시험 제도의 변화	81
Topic_13	**The Formation Of N sync** '엔 씽크' 뮤직 밴드의 형성	87
Topic_14	**Stay Away From Soda Pop!** 소다수 음료를 멀리 하자!	93
Topic_15	**A Fantasy Can Become A Reality** 공상 소설이 현실로 되다	99

Contents

LEVEL 2

Topic_01	**Walt Disney Will Bring Joy Into Our Lives Forever** 월트 디즈니는 우리의 삶속에 기쁨을 영언히 가져다줄 것이다	107
Topic_02	**Be Aware Of The Global Warming!** 지구온난화를 경계하라!	113
Topic_03	**Fight Off The Cold** 추위를 이겨내자	119
Topic_04	**Decorate My Pasta!** 파스타를 장식하자!	125
Topic_05	**The Best Ways To Make The Best Jack-O'-Lantern** 최고의 호박등을 만드는 최상의 방법	131
Topic_06	**Save The Koala Bears** 코알라를 보호하자	137
Topic_07	**Volleyball On The Sand** 모래 위에서 하는 배구	143
Topic_08	**The Rising Popularity Of The Japanese Animated Films** 인기 폭등하고 있는 일본 만화 영화	149
Topic_09	**The True Football Fans Exist In America** 진정한 미식축구 팬은 미국에 있다	155
Topic_10	**Craving For A Hot Dog?** 핫도그 먹고 싶으세요?	161
Topic_11	**Students Want To Show Their Own Styles** 학생들은 자기들만의 스타일을 보여 주기를 원한다	167
Topic_12	**Vegetables Are Good For Cars Too!** 야채는 자동차에게도 중요하다!	173
Topic_13	**The Olympic Games Will Be Treasured Forever** 올림픽 게임은 영원한 가치를 지닌다	179
Topic_14	**Fly Up In A Hot Air Balloon** 열기구를 타고 하늘로 날아오르자	185
Topic_15	**Flying Mammals** 날아다니는 포유동물	191

LEVEL 3

Topic_01	**Do You Know Who Philip Ahn Is?** 필립 안이 누구인지 아나요?		199
Topic_02	**Deja Vu** 데자뷰		205
Topic_03	**Some Facts About Penguins** 펭귄에 대한 사실들		211
Topic_04	**The Invention Of The E-mail** 이메일의 출현		217
Topic_05	**Fashion Trends** 패션 트렌드		223
Topic_06	**Fall In Love** 사랑에 빠지다		229
Topic_07	**Fish That Break Wind** 방귀 뀌는 물고기		235
Topic_08	**The Colorful Rainbow** 화려한 무지개		241
Topic_09	**The Blue Sky** 파란 하늘		247
Topic_10	**The Importance Of Water** 물의 중요성		253
Topic_11	**Natural Foods Prevent Us From Getting Sick** 자연식품이 질병을 예방한다		259
Topic_12	**Alfred Nobel** 알프레드 노벨		265
Topic_13	**The Bridal Shower** 신부 파티		271
Topic_14	**Get Away From The Indoor Air Pollutants** 실내 공기 오염물을 퇴치하자		277
Topic_15	**What Is A Piggy Bank?** 돼지 저금통이란?		283

READ ALOUD

LEVEL 1

LEVEL 1

Topic no.	Title
01	Wearing Backpacks Could Be Harmful
02	Harry Potter Is Truly Popular
03	The Junior High School Education System In Canada
04	Let's Dance And Study
05	Save The Leatherback Sea Turtle!
06	Hot Dogs For Americans
07	Read "Peanuts" And Laugh!
08	Cars Are Valuable Everywhere
09	Babies Prefer Beautiful People
10	From Comic Books To The Screen
11	Join The Girl Scouts Now!
12	Middle School Entrance Exam Changes
13	The Formation Of N sync
14	Stay Away From Soda Pop!
15	A Fantasy Can Become A Reality

Topic 01

LEVEL 1

WEARING BACKPACKS COULD BE HARMFUL

배낭을 메고 다니는 것은 위험할 수 있다

Step ❶

Understanding

음원을 들으면서 눈으로 읽어 보고,
문제를 통해서 이해했는지 확인해 보세요.

Backpacks can be dangerous because they can hurt people's backs. Doctors know this well. However, many American teenagers still carry a backpack to school. In fact, 40 million teenagers in the U.S. carry a backpack to school. Doctors and parents are worried about this.

 윗글의 주제가 되도록 빈칸을 채워 보자.

Problems with _____ for teenagers.

Voca. ▪ million 100만　　▪ back 허리

Step ❷

Listening

이번에는 억양과 끊어 읽기, 연음과 강조어에 대한 강의를 들어 보세요.

/ 끊어 읽기   ∫↘ 억양   **볼드색 강세를 두어 읽는 부분**   ⌣ 연음

Backpacks can‿be dangerous **because** / they can ∫hurt people's‿backs.

Doctors ↘ know this‿well.

However, / many American teenagers / still carry‿a backpack to ↘school.

In fact, / 40 million teenagers in‿the U.S. / carry‿a backpack to school.

Doctors **and** parents‿are ∫worried‿about this.

Step ❸

Read Slowly

스스로 끊어 읽기와 억양을 직접 표시하면서,
천천히 큰 소리로 읽어 보세요.

1회 □   2회 □   3회 □   4회 □   5회 □   6회 □   7회 □

Backpacks can be dangerous because they can hurt people's backs.

Doctors know this well.

However, many American teenagers still carry a backpack to school.

In fact, 40 million teenagers in the U.S. carry a backpack to school.

Doctors and parents are worried about this.

Step ④

Read Normal Speed with shadowing

자신이 생겼다면 이제 내용을 전달하면서 큰 소리로 따라 읽어 보세요.

1회 □   2회 □   3회 □   4회 □   5회 □   6회 □   7회 □

Step ⑤

Speak / Presentation

이제는 아래 글을 완성하면서 큰 소리로 사람들 앞에서 발표해 보세요.

Backpacks can be dangerous because they ____ ____ _____ _____. Doctors ____ ____ well. _____, _____ _____ _____ still carry a backpack to school. In fact, 40 million teenagers ____ ____ U.S. _____ __ backpack to school. Doctors and parents ____ _____ ____ ____.

○ Script

배낭은 등에 무리를 줄 수 있기 때문에 위험할 수 있다. 의사들은 이 사실을 잘 안다. 그러나 많은 미국 십대들은 여전히 배낭을 매고 학교에 간다. 사실, 미국의 4천 만 십대들이 배낭을 매고 학교를 다닌다. 의사들과 부모들은 이 사실을 염려하고 있다.

● 정답 > Problems with **backpacks** for teenagers.

Take a break

▶ 영어발음을 향상시키는 방법

can과 can't를 말해 보세요!

우리들이 영어로 말할 때 정확하게 발음을 잘 하지 못하는 단어가 많이 있습니다. 그 중에서도 자주 틀리는 발음을 하는 단어가 바로 can't입니다. 가끔, 한국인들이 I can't.라고 했을 때 많은 미국인들이 I can.이라고 말한 것과 혼동할 때가 많습니다. 이런 경우에는, can't 끝 부분을 조금 더 강조해서 분명히 들리게 해야 합니다. 특히, t 발음을 조금 강조하면, 듣는 사람이 좀 더 확실하게 어떤 말을 했는지 이해할 수 있습니다. can과 can't의 경우 발음에 따라 의미를 아주 다르게 전달할 수 있는 단어이므로 끝 부분을 정확히 발음해서 의사 전달이 제대로 이루어지도록 하세요.

Topic 02

LEVEL 1

HARRY POTTER IS TRULY POPULAR

해리포터는 인기 절정

Step ❶

Understanding

음원을 들으면서 눈으로 읽어 보고,
문제를 통해서 이해했는지 확인해 보세요.

J. K. Rowling's Harry Potter series is popular in bookstores around the world. For example, in America there are almost 80 million Harry Potter books! Children love Harry Potter because of the magic and fantasy. Adults love Harry Potter because of the action and adventure.

윗글의 주제로 삼기에 가장 알맞은 것은?
ⓐ J. K. Rowling
ⓑ Harry Potter series
ⓒ Books
ⓓ Bookstores

- popular 인기 있는
- fantasy 상상, 공상
- adventure 모험

Step ❷

Listening

이번에는 억양과 끊어 읽기, 연음과 강조어에 대한
강의를 들어 보세요.

/ 끊어 읽기   ∫↘ 억양   **볼드색** 강세를 두어 읽는 부분   ‿ 연음

J. K. Rowling's Harry Potter series / is popular‿in bookstores ∫
around the world.

For example, / in‿America there ↘are‿almost 80 **million**
Harry Potter books!

Children **love** Harry Potter ↘because of‿the magic **and** ↘
fantasy.

Adults‿love Harry Potter / because of the action **and**
adventure.

Step ❸

Read Slowly

스스로 끊어 읽기와 억양을 직접 표시하면서,
천천히 큰 소리로 읽어 보세요.

1회 □   2회 □   3회 □   4회 □   5회 □   6회 □   7회 □

J. K. Rowling's Harry Potter series is popular in bookstores around the world.

For example, in America there are almost 80 million Harry Potter books!

Children love Harry Potter because of the magic and fantasy.

Adults love Harry Potter because of the action and adventure.

Step ❹

Read Normal Speed with shadowing

자신이 생겼다면 이제 내용을 전달하면서 큰 소리로 따라 읽어 보세요.

1회 ☐   2회 ☐   3회 ☐   4회 ☐   5회 ☐   6회 ☐   7회 ☐

Step ❺

Speak / Presentation

이제는 아래 글을 완성하면서 큰 소리로 사람들 앞에서 발표해 보세요.

J. K. Rowling's Harry Potter series _____ _____ ___ bookstores around the world. For example, ___ _____ there are almost 80 million Harry Potter books! Children love Harry Potter because ___ _____ _____ _____ _____. Adults love Harry Potter _____ ___ _____ action and adventure.

○ Script

조앤 롤링(J. K. Rowling)의 해리포터 시리즈는 전 세계 서점의 인기 도서이다. 예를 들면, 미국에서는 해리포터 책이 거의 8천만 부가 나왔다. 아이들은 해리포터가 마법과 환상의 소설이기 때문에 좋아하고, 성인들은 해리포터가 액션과 모험의 소설이기 때문에 좋아한다.

● 정답 > b. Harry Potter series

Take a break

▶ 영어발음을 향상시키는 방법

입을 크게 벌리고 말해 보세요!

영어 단어들을 읽거나 영어로 말을 할 때에는 한국말과 다르게 입과 입 모양을 생각하며 신중하게 말해야 합니다. 특히, 한국말은 입과 입술을 많이 움직이지 않지만 영어로 말을 할 때에는 더 정확한 소리를 내기 위해서 입과 입술을 좀 더 크게 움직여서 말을 해야 합니다.

Topic 03   LEVEL 1

THE JUNIOR HIGH SCHOOL EDUCATION SYSTEM IN CANADA

캐나다의 중등 교육 제도

Step ❶

Understanding

음원을 들으면서 눈으로 읽어 보고,
문제를 통해서 이해했는지 확인해 보세요.

In Canada, junior high school is only two years long, grades 7 and 8. Students start school at 9:00 a.m. They have three subjects in the morning and then one hour for lunch. In the afternoon, they have another three subjects. School usually ends around 3:30 p.m. After school, a lot of students play sports. Some students play on school sports teams and other students play sports for fun.

 윗글의 주제로 가장 알맞은 것은?
ⓐ Canadian junior high schools
ⓑ Junior high school students
ⓒ The class schedule
ⓓ After-school sports

 ▪ junior high school 중학교   ▪ grade 학년   ▪ subject 과목

Step ❷

Listening

이번에는 억양과 끊어 읽기, 연음과 강조어에 대한 강의를 들어 보세요.

/ 끊어 읽기　∫↘ 억양　**볼드색** 강세를 두어 읽는 부분　‿ 연음

In Canada, / junior high school is‿only two years long, / grades 7 and 8.

Students ∫start school at‿9:00 a.m.

They ↘have / three subjects in‿the morning / and‿then ∫ one hour‿for lunch.

In the ∫afternoon, / they have ∫another‿three subjects.

School **usually** ↘ends‿around 3:30 p.m.

After school, / **a lot**‿of students / play ↘sports.

Some students play‿on school sports teams / and‿other students play ∫sports for fun.

Step ❸

Read Slowly

스스로 끊어 읽기와 억양을 직접 표시하면서,
천천히 큰 소리로 읽어 보세요.

1회 □ 2회 □ 3회 □ 4회 □ 5회 □ 6회 □ 7회 □

In Canada, junior high school is only two years long, grades 7 and 8.

Students start school at 9:00 a.m.

They have three subjects in the morning and then one hour for lunch.

In the afternoon, they have another three subjects.

School usually ends around 3:30 p.m.

After school, a lot of students play sports.

Some students play on school sports teams and other students play sports for fun.

Step ❹

Read Normal Speed with shadowing

자신이 생겼다면 이제 내용을 전달하면서 큰 소리로 따라 읽어 보세요.

1회 □ 2회 □ 3회 □ 4회 □ 5회 □ 6회 □ 7회 □

Step ❺

Speak / Presentation

이제는 아래 글을 완성하면서 큰 소리로 사람들 앞에서 발표해 보세요.

In Canada, junior high school is ____ ___ _____ ____, grades 7 and 8. Students _____ _____ ___ 9:00 a.m. They have three subjects ___ ___ _____ and then one hour for lunch. In the afternoon, ____ _____ _____ _____ subjects. School _____ ____ _____ 3:30 p.m. After school, a lot of students _____ _____. Some students play on school sports teams and other students play _____ ___ ____.

○ Script

캐나다에서 중학교 과정은 7학년과 8학년의 2개 학년뿐이다. 수업은 오전 9시에 시작한다. 학생들은 오전에 3과목을 듣고, 한 시간의 점심시간을 갖는다. 오후에는 다른 3과목을 듣는다. 보통 학교는 3시 반쯤 끝나는데 방과 후에는 많은 학생들이 운동을 한다. 어떤 학생들은 학교 운동 팀에 속해 운동을 하고 다른 학생들은 재미삼아 운동을 한다.

● 정답 〉 a. Canadian junior high schools

Take a break

▶ 영어발음을 향상시키는 방법

f와 v 발음

많은 한국 사람들이 f와 v 발음을 잘 구분하지 못합니다. 여러분들도 그런 문제가 있으신가요? 한번 해 보세요! 어떤 발음이 잘 안 된다고 느낀다면 거울 앞에 가서 입 모양을 한번 쳐다보면서 발음을 해 보세요. f 발음을 할 때에는 위의 앞 이빨로 아랫입술을 살짝 깨무는 것처럼 하고 발음을 해야 합니다. 그리고 힘을 좀 더 주면서 발음을 해 보세요.

Topic 04

LEVEL 1

LET'S DANCE AND STUDY

공부도 하고 춤도 추자

Step ❶

Understanding

음원을 들으면서 눈으로 읽어 보고,
문제를 통해서 이해했는지 확인해 보세요.

Students in the United States like to go to school dances. Dancing is very popular. From grade seven, when students are 12 years old, schools host dances. School dances usually begin at 7:00 p.m. They often finish at 12:00 a.m. After the dance, sometimes boys and girls exchange phone numbers. Later, they can go on a date together.

Q! 윗글의 주제로 가장 알맞은 것은?
ⓐ Students in the U.S.
ⓑ Junior high school
ⓒ School dances
ⓓ Popular dancing

 • host 주최하다　• exchange 교환하다

Step ❷

Listening

이번에는 억양과 끊어 읽기, 연음과 강조어에 대한 강의를 들어 보세요.

/ 끊어 읽기   ∫ ⌡ 억양   **볼드색** 강세를 두어 읽는 부분   ⌣ 연음

Students in‿the United States / **like** to go to ⌡school dances.

Dancing ⌡is **very** popular.

From grade seven, / when students are 12 years old, / schools ∫host dances.

School dances / usually begin‿at 7:00 p.m.

They‿often finish / at 12:00 a.m.

After‿the dance, / **sometimes** boys and ∫girls exchange phone numbers.

Later, / they can‿go on a date ∫together.

Step ❸

Read Slowly

스스로 끊어 읽기와 억양을 직접 표시하면서,
천천히 큰 소리로 읽어 보세요.

1회 ☐   2회 ☐   3회 ☐   4회 ☐   5회 ☐   6회 ☐   7회 ☐

Students in the United States like to go to school dances.

Dancing is very popular.

From grade seven, when students are 12 years old, schools host dances.

School dances usually begin at 7:00 p.m.

They often finish at 12:00 a.m.

After the dance, sometimes boys and girls exchange phone numbers.

Later, they can go on a date together.

Step ④

Read Normal Speed with shadowing

자신이 생겼다면 이제 내용을 전달하면서 큰 소리로 따라 읽어 보세요.

1회 ☐   2회 ☐   3회 ☐   4회 ☐   5회 ☐   6회 ☐   7회 ☐

Step ⑤

Speak / Presentation

이제는 아래 글을 완성하면서 큰 소리로 사람들 앞에서 발표해 보세요.

Students in the United States like __ __ __ _____ _____. _____ __ very popular. From grade seven, when students are 12 years old, _____ _____ dances. School dances _____ _____ __ 7:00 p.m. _____ _____ _____ at 12:00 a.m. After the dance, sometimes boys _____ _____ _____ phone numbers. Later, they can __ __ __ _____ together.

Level 1 • 37

○ Script

미국 학생들은 학교 댄스파티에 가는 것을 좋아한다. 댄스파티는 매우 인기가 있다. 학생들이 12살이 되는 7학년부터 학교에서 댄스파티를 주최한다. 학교 댄스파티는 보통 오후 7시에 시작해서 종종 밤 12시에 끝난다. 댄스파티가 끝난 후 때로는 남자아이들과 여자아이들은 서로의 전화번호를 교환하기도 한다. 나중에 그들은 함께 데이트를 갈 수도 있다.

- 정답 > c. School dances

Take a break

▶ 영어발음을 향상시키는 방법

b와 v 발음

대부분의 한국 사람들은 b 발음을 아주 잘합니다. 그러나 가끔 b 발음과 v 발음을 정확하게 구분하지 못해서 상대방이 잘못 알아듣는 경우가 있습니다. v 발음을 해야 하는데 b 발음으로 사용하는 경우가 대부분이죠. 예를 들면, vacuum을 [배큠]이라고 b 발음을 해서 말합니다. v 발음을 할 때에는 윗니를 아랫입술에 살짝 대면서 발음을 하면 됩니다.

Topic 05 LEVEL 1

SAVE THE LEATHERBACK SEA TURTLE!

BY RYAN O HARE

바다 장수거북이를 살리자!

Step ❶

Understanding

음원을 들으면서 눈으로 읽어 보고,
문제를 통해서 이해했는지 확인해 보세요.

Leatherback sea turtles were alive during the dinosaur age. They survived the ice ages. Now, they are endangered animals. Over the last 20 years, the number of leatherback sea turtles has fallen by 95 percent. If governments don't take action soon, this ancient turtle may soon be found only in history books.

Q! 윗글을 읽고 다음 빈칸을 채우시오.
Leatherback sea turtles survived the _____ _____ and the _____ _____.

- leatherback sea turtle 장수거북이
- dinosaur 공룡
- ancient 고대의

Step ❷

Listening

이번에는 억양과 끊어 읽기, 연음과 강조어에 대한 강의를 들어 보세요.

/ 끊어 읽기   ∫ ↘ 억양   **볼드색 강세를 두어 읽는 부분**   ‿ 연음

Leatherback sea turtles were **alive** during‿the dinosaur ↘ age.

They ∫ survived the ice ages.

Now, / they ↘ are **endangered** animals.

Over‿the ∫ last 20 years, / the number‿of leatherback sea turtles / has ↘ fallen **by** 95 percent.

If governments don't take action ∫ soon, / this ancient turtle / may‿**soon** be found **only**‿in history ↘ books.

Step ❸

Read Slowly

스스로 끊어 읽기와 억양을 직접 표시하면서,
천천히 큰 소리로 읽어 보세요.

| 1회 □ | 2회 □ | 3회 □ | 4회 □ | 5회 □ | 6회 □ | 7회 □ |

Leatherback sea turtles were alive during the dinosaur age.

They survived the ice ages.

Now, they are endangered animals.

Over the last 20 years, the number of leatherback sea turtles has fallen by 95 percent.

If governments don't take action soon, this ancient turtle may soon be found only in history books.

Step ❹

Read Normal Speed with shadowing
자신이 생겼다면 이제 내용을 전달하면서 큰 소리로 따라 읽어 보세요.

1회 □ 2회 □ 3회 □ 4회 □ 5회 □ 6회 □ 7회 □

Step ❺

Speak / Presentation
이제는 아래 글을 완성하면서 큰 소리로 사람들 앞에서 발표해 보세요.

Leatherback sea turtles were alive _____ _____ _____ _____. They survived the _____ _____. Now, _____ _____ _____ animals. _____ _____ _____ 20 years, the number of leatherback sea turtles has fallen by 95 percent. If governments don't take action soon, _____ _____ _____ _____ _____ be found only in history books.

○ Script

장수거북이는 공룡 시대에도 있었고, 빙하기에도 살아남았다. 지금은 멸종 위기의 동물이 되었다. 지난 20년 동안 장수거북이 수는 95퍼센트까지 감소했다. 정부가 조속히 어떤 조치를 취하지 않으면, 얼마 지나지 않아 고대로부터 살아남은 이 거북이는 아마 역사책 속에서나 찾을 수 있게 될 것이다.

- 정답 > Leatherback sea turtles survived the **dinosaur age** and the **ice ages**.

Take a break

▶ 영어발음을 향상시키는 방법

t 발음

여러분들 대부분은 t 발음을 할 때 어려움이 있으시죠? 물론 없다면 다행입니다. 하지만 보통 t 발음을 가벼운 d 발음으로 소리 낼 때가 많습니다. 예를 들어, sit을 발음할 때 t 발음을 강하게 하지 않고, 가볍게 d와 t 발음의 중간 소리를 만드는 경우가 있습니다. 물론 완전한 d도 아닙니다. 단어의 끝에 오는 t는 그냥 소리를 가볍게 만든다고 생각하면 됩니다. 그러나 예를 들어, take처럼 t가 단어의 처음에 올 때는 좀 강하게 t 발음을 해 주는 것이 좋습니다.

Topic 06   LEVEL 1

HOT DOGS FOR AMERICANS

미국인과 핫도그

Step ❶

Understanding

음원을 들으면서 눈으로 읽어 보고,
문제를 통해서 이해했는지 확인해 보세요.

How much do Americans love hot dogs? More than you can probably imagine. Hot dogs are sold on streets, in supermarkets, and at sports events. Plus, Americans make them at home, especially on holidays. Did you know that Americans eat about 150 million hot dogs on Independence Day(July 4)? During the summer, Americans eat 7 billion hot dogs! Americans really love to eat hot dogs.

 윗글의 요지로 가장 알맞은 것은?
ⓐ Americans can buy hot dogs in different places.
ⓑ Americans really like to eat hot dogs.
ⓒ Americans eat many hot dogs in summer.
ⓓ Americans can make hot dogs.

 • Independence Day 독립기념일

Step ❷

Listening

이번에는 억양과 끊어 읽기, 연음과 강조어에 대한 강의를 들어 보세요.

/ 끊어 읽기   ∫ ⌡ 억양   **볼드색 강세를 두어 읽는 부분**   ‿ 연음

How ∫**much** do Americans **love** hot dogs? ⌡

More ⌡than you can probably imagine.

Hot dogs are sold‿on streets, / in supermarkets, / **and** at sports events.

Plus, / Americans make‿them at home, / **especially** ⌡on holidays.

Did ∫you know / that Americans eat about **150 million** hot dogs / on Independence Day(July 4)? ∫

During‿the summer, / Americans eat ∫7 billion **hot dogs**!

Americans **really** love to‿eat hot dogs.

Step ❸ MP3

Read Slowly

스스로 끊어 읽기와 억양을 직접 표시하면서,
천천히 큰 소리로 읽어 보세요.

1회 ☐　2회 ☐　3회 ☐　4회 ☐　5회 ☐　6회 ☐　7회 ☐

How much do Americans love hot dogs?

More than you can probably imagine.

Hot dogs are sold on streets, in supermarkets, and at sports events.

Plus, Americans make them at home, especially on holidays.

Did you know that Americans eat about 150 million hot dogs on Independence Day(July 4)?

During the summer, Americans eat 7 billion hot dogs!

Americans really love to eat hot dogs.

Step ❹

Read Normal Speed with shadowing

자신이 생겼다면 이제 내용을 전달하면서 큰 소리로 따라 읽어 보세요.

| 1회 ☐ | 2회 ☐ | 3회 ☐ | 4회 ☐ | 5회 ☐ | 6회 ☐ | 7회 ☐ |

Step ❺

Speak / Presentation

이제는 아래 글을 완성하면서 큰 소리로 사람들 앞에서 발표해 보세요.

____ ____ ____ Americans love hot dogs? More than you can _____ _____. Hot dogs ____ ____ __ streets, in supermarkets, and at sports events. Plus, Americans ____ ____ __ ____, especially on holidays. Did you know that _____ ____ ____ 150 million hot dogs on Independence Day(July 4)? _____ ____ _____, Americans eat 7 billion hot dogs! Americans ____ ____ __ eat hot dogs.

○ Script

미국인들은 핫도그를 얼마나 좋아할까? 아마도 당신이 상상하는 그 이상일 것이다. 핫도그는 길거리, 슈퍼마켓 그리고 스포츠 행사장에서 판매된다. 게다가, 휴일에는 미국인들이 집에서도 핫도그를 만든다. 미국인들이 독립기념일(7월 4일)에 약 1억 5천만 개나 되는 핫도그를 먹는다는 것을 알고 있는가? 여름 동안 미국인들은 70억 개의 핫도그를 먹는다! 미국인들은 정말로 핫도그를 좋아한다.

- **정답** > b. Americans really like to eat hot dogs.

Take a break

▶ 영어발음을 향상시키는 방법

t 발음에 관한 주의점

어떤 때에는 t가 ch 소리를 낼 때가 있습니다. 예를 들어 train을 발음할 때 [t-rain]이 아니라 chocolate할 때 ch 발음으로 [ch-rain]이라고 합니다. tree의 경우도 마찬가지입니다. 보통 tr로 시작하는 단어들을 발음할 때 실수를 하는 경우가 많은데 주의하세요.

Topic 07

LEVEL 1

READ "PEANUTS" AND LAUGH!

만화 "피너츠"를 보고 웃어 보자!

Step ❶

Understanding

음원을 들으면서 눈으로 읽어 보고,
문제를 통해서 이해했는지 확인해 보세요.

"Peanuts" is a world famous comic. Charles Schulz created "Peanuts" with lovable characters like Snoopy, Woodstock, Lucy and Charlie Brown. "Peanuts" was in only seven daily newspapers in the U.S. in 1950. Today, the "Peanuts" is in thousands of newspapers around the world. It will always be many people's favorite comic.

 윗글의 요지로 알맞은 것은?

ⓐ Charles Schulz was a world famous cartoonist.
ⓑ Peanuts is a comic.
ⓒ Peanuts was first published in 1950.
ⓓ Peanuts will always be many people's favorite comic.

 · comic 만화

Step ❷

Listening

이번에는 억양과 끊어 읽기, 연음과 강조어에 대한 강의를 들어 보세요.

/ 끊어 읽기　↗↘ 억양　**볼드색 강세를 두어 읽는 부분**　‿ 연음

"Peanuts" / is a world famous ↘comic.

Charles Schulz created ↗"Peanuts" with **lovable** characters like / Snoopy, / Woodstock, / Lucy / and Charlie Brown.

"Peanuts" was in‿**only** seven daily newspapers in‿the U.S. in ↘1950.

Today, / the "Peanuts" is‿in **thousands of** newspapers ↗ around the ↘world.

It will‿always be **many** people's favorite comic.

Step ❸

Read Slowly

스스로 끊어 읽기와 억양을 직접 표시하면서,
천천히 큰 소리로 읽어 보세요.

1회 ☐ 2회 ☐ 3회 ☐ 4회 ☐ 5회 ☐ 6회 ☐ 7회 ☐

"Peanuts" is a world famous comic.

Charles Schulz created "Peanuts" with lovable characters like Snoopy, Woodstock, Lucy and Charlie Brown.

"Peanuts" was in only seven daily newspapers in the U.S. in 1950.

Today, the "Peanuts" is in thousands of newspapers around the world.

It will always be many people's favorite comic.

Step ④

Read Normal Speed with shadowing

자신이 생겼다면 이제 내용을 전달하면서 큰 소리로 따라 읽어 보세요.

1회 □   2회 □   3회 □   4회 □   5회 □   6회 □   7회 □

Step ⑤

Speak / Presentation

이제는 아래 글을 완성하면서 큰 소리로 사람들 앞에서 발표해 보세요.

"Peanuts" is ___ _____ _____ comic. Charles Schulz created "Peanuts" with _____ _____ like Snoopy, Woodstock, Lucy and Charlie Brown. "Peanuts" was in _____ _____ _____ newspapers in the U.S. in 1950. Today, the "Peanuts" _____ ___ _____ ___ newspapers around the world. It will always be many people's _____ _____.

Script

'피너츠'는 전 세계적으로 유명한 만화이다. 찰스 슐츠는 '피너츠'에서 스누피, 우드스탁, 루시, 그리고 찰리 브라운과 같은 사랑스러운 캐릭터들을 만들어 냈다. 1950년에 '피너츠'는 미국에서 겨우 7개의 일간지에만 실렸다. 오늘날은 전 세계 수천 종의 신문에 연재되고 있다. '피너츠'는 언제나 많은 사람들이 가장 좋아하는 만화로 남을 것이다.

● 정답 > d. Peanuts will always be many people's favorite comic.

Take a break

▶ 영어발음을 향상시키는 방법

-tion 발음에 관한 아주 중요한 포인트

대부분 한국 사람들은 [션]이라고 발음하면서 말을 하는데, 절대로 이 발음이 아닙니다! 모두들 조심하시기 바랍니다. 듣는 사람들이 이해는 하겠지만 무척 어색하고 자연스럽게 들리지 않습니다. 바른 발음은 [sh-in]입니다. 그럼 concentration을 읽어 보세요! 모든 -tion을 이런 식으로 발음해야 합니다.

Topic 08

LEVEL 1

CARS ARE VALUABLE EVERYWHERE

자동차는 어디에서나 중요하다

Step ❶

Understanding

음원을 들으면서 눈으로 읽어 보고,
문제를 통해서 이해했는지 확인해 보세요.

Americans use their cars a lot. Today, Americans use automobiles for more than 90 percent of their daily trips. An average person drives more than 9,000 miles a year. Forty years ago, Americans drove only 4,000 miles a year. These days, the average driver spends 443 hours a year behind the steering wheel. That's nearly twenty days a year!

*1 mile = 2.2 kilometers

 윗글의 요지로 알맞은 것은?
ⓐ Americans drive very much.
ⓑ Americans are tired of driving too much.
ⓒ Americans drive a few times a year.
ⓓ Americans are driving less every year.

 ▪ automobile 자동차 ▪ trip 통근 ▪ average 평균

Step ❷

Listening

이번에는 억양과 끊어 읽기, 연음과 강조어에 대한 강의를 들어 보세요.

/ 끊어 읽기   ⌒ 억양   **볼드색** 강세를 두어 읽는 부분   ‿ 연음

Americans use‿their cars **a lot**.

Today, / Americans use automobiles / for ⌒more than **90 percent** of‿their daily trips.

An ⌒average person drives **more than** 9,000 miles a year.

Forty years ago, / Americans drove **only** 4,000 miles a year.

These ⌒days, / the **average** driver spends 443 hours a year / behind‿the steering wheel.

That's ⌒nearly **twenty** days a year! ⌒

Step ❸

Read Slowly

스스로 끊어 읽기와 억양을 직접 표시하면서,
천천히 큰 소리로 읽어 보세요.

1회 □ 2회 □ 3회 □ 4회 □ 5회 □ 6회 □ 7회 □

Americans use their cars a lot.

Today, Americans use automobiles for more than 90 percent of their daily trips.

An average person drives more than 9,000 miles a year.

Forty years ago, Americans drove only 4,000 miles a year.

These days, the average driver spends 443 hours a year behind the steering wheel.

That's nearly twenty days a year!

Step ❹

Read Normal Speed with shadowing
자신이 생겼다면 이제 내용을 전달하면서 큰 소리로 따라 읽어 보세요.

| 1회 ☐ | 2회 ☐ | 3회 ☐ | 4회 ☐ | 5회 ☐ | 6회 ☐ | 7회 ☐ |

Step ❺

Speak / Presentation
이제는 아래 글을 완성하면서 큰 소리로 사람들 앞에서 발표해 보세요.

Americans ____ ____ ____ a lot. Today, Americans use automobiles for more than 90 percent ___ ____ _____ ____. An average _____ _____ ____ ____ 9,000 miles a year. Forty years ago, Americans _____ ____ 4,000 miles a year. These days, the average driver spends 443 hours a year ____ ____ _____ ____. That's nearly _____ ____ ___ ____!

○ Script

미국인들은 자동차를 많이 이용한다. 오늘날 미국인들은 하루 통근량의 90% 이상을 자동차로 이용한다. 평균적으로 한 사람당 1년에 9천 마일 이상을 운전한다. 40년 전 미국인들은 1년에 단지 4천 마일을 운전하였다. 오늘날 보통 운전자는 1년에 443시간을 핸들 뒤에서 보내고 있다. 이는 1년 중 거의 20일에 해당하는 것이다!

*1 마일 = 2.2 킬로미터

- **정답** > a. Americans drive very much.

Take a break

▶ 영어발음을 향상시키는 방법

여러분은 mint 캔디를 좋아하십니까?

보통 -ment로 끝나는 영어 단어들이 많죠? 어떻게 발음하십니까? 예를 들어, comment 혹은 arrangement라고 할 때, 많은 한국인들이 끝부분을 [맨트]라고 발음하는데 그렇지 않습니다. ment는 mint처럼 짧게 i 발음에 가깝게 하는 것이 자연스럽습니다.

Topic 09

LEVEL 1

BABIES PREFER BEAUTIFUL PEOPLE

아기들은 아름다운 사람들을 좋아한다

Step ❶

Understanding

음원을 들으면서 눈으로 읽어 보고,
문제를 통해서 이해했는지 확인해 보세요.

Most people believe that we learn what beauty is as we grow up. But, new research shows it is not true. Researchers held two pictures in front of babies, from one to seven days, for 30 seconds. On one picture was an ugly person; on the other picture was a beautiful person. More often, babies looked at the beautiful person's picture longer. The conclusion: we are born with an idea of what beauty is.

 윗글의 요지로 알맞은 것은?

ⓐ Babies are born with an idea of what beauty is.
ⓑ We learn what beauty is as we grow up.
ⓒ Babies don't know about beauty.
ⓓ We learn about beauty later on in life.

- researcher 연구원, 연구자
- held 들고 있었다, hold의 과거형

Step ❷

Listening

이번에는 억양과 끊어 읽기, 연음과 강조어에 대한 강의를 들어 보세요.

/ 끊어 읽기   ∫ ↘ 억양   **볼드색** 강세를 두어 읽는 부분   ‿ 연음

Most people ∫ believe that we learn what beauty is as‿we grow up.

But, / **new** research ∫ shows it is not ↘ true.

Researchers held **two** pictures in‿front of babies, / from one to ↘ seven days, / for 30 seconds.

On one picture / was an **ugly** person; / on‿the ∫ other picture / was a **beautiful** person.

More often, / babies ↘ looked at‿the beautiful person's picture longer.

The conclusion: / we ∫ are born with‿an idea of what beauty ↘ is.

Step ❸

 **Read Slowly**

스스로 끊어 읽기와 억양을 직접 표시하면서,
천천히 큰 소리로 읽어 보세요.

1회 □ 2회 □ 3회 □ 4회 □ 5회 □ 6회 □ 7회 □

Most people believe that we learn what beauty is as we grow up.

But, new research shows it is not true.

Researchers held two pictures in front of babies, from one to seven days, for 30 seconds.

On one picture was an ugly person; on the other picture was a beautiful person.

More often, babies looked at the beautiful person's picture longer.

The conclusion: we are born with an idea of what beauty is.

Step ❹

Read Normal Speed with shadowing

자신이 생겼다면 이제 내용을 전달하면서 큰 소리로 따라 읽어 보세요.

1회 ☐ 2회 ☐ 3회 ☐ 4회 ☐ 5회 ☐ 6회 ☐ 7회 ☐

Step ❺

Speak / Presentation

이제는 아래 글을 완성하면서 큰 소리로 사람들 앞에서 발표해 보세요.

Most people believe that we learn what beauty is ___ ___ ___ ___. But, new ___ ___ ___ ___ not true. Researchers held two ___ ___ ___ ___ babies, from one to seven days, for 30 seconds. ___ ___ ___ ___ an ugly person; on the other picture was a beautiful person. More often, ___ ___ ___ ___ beautiful person's picture longer. The conclusion: we are born with an idea of ___ ___ ___.

○ Script

대부분의 사람들은 우리가 성장하면서 아름다움이 무엇인지를 알게 된다고 믿고 있다. 하지만, 새로운 연구 결과에 따르면 사실은 그렇지 않다. 연구자들은 생후 1일에서 7일 된 신생아들 앞에 30초간 2가지 사진을 들고 있었다. 한 사진에는 못생긴 사람이, 다른 사진에는 아름다운 사람이 있었다. 여러 차례 신생아들은 아름다운 사람의 사진을 더 오랫동안 쳐다보았다. 결국, 우리는 아름다움에 대한 개념을 갖고 태어난다는 결론에 도달한다.

* 탄야 랜돌이 '사이언스 미러'에 한 특별 기고

● **정답** > a. Babies are born with an idea of what beauty is.

Take a break

▶ 영어발음을 향상시키는 방법

r 발음

우리들이 많이 힘들어 하는 발음에는 r이 들어간 단어가 많습니다. 이 r 발음을 향상시키기 위해서 red rose을 몇 번 해 보세요. 쉬울 수도 있지만 매우 힘들 수도 있습니다. r이 단어의 첫 스펠링으로 올 때는 입술을 중간으로 모아야 하고, 윗니와 아랫입술을 살짝 대면서 발음을 해야 합니다. r이 중간이나 단어의 끝에 올 때는 이빨이 아랫입술에 닿지 않도록, 그냥 위아래 입술을 모은 상태로 소리를 내면 됩니다.

Topic 10

LEVEL 1

FROM COMIC BOOKS TO THE SCREEN

만화책이 영화가 되다

Step ❶

Understanding

음원을 들으면서 눈으로 읽어 보고,
문제를 통해서 이해했는지 확인해 보세요.

It's not uncommon for movies to come from comic books. You might know some famous examples like *Spiderman*, *Superman*, and *X-Men*. There are many other cases of movies coming from comic books. The followings are a few recent examples of comics turned into movies:

Blade   Hellboy   Hulk   The mask   Men in black

 윗글의 주제로 가장 알맞은 것은?
ⓐ Comic movies
ⓑ Popular comic books
ⓒ Children's favorite comic books
ⓓ Movies that came from comic books

- turn into ~로 변하다

Step ❷

Listening

이번에는 억양과 끊어 읽기, 연음과 강조어에 대한 강의를 들어 보세요.

/ 끊어 읽기   ∫ ↘ 억양   **볼드색** 강세를 두어 읽는 부분   ‿ 연음

It's **not** uncommon for movies to ∫ come from comic books.

You ∫ might know some famous examples like / *Spiderman*, / *Superman*, / and *X-Men*.

There are **many** other cases ↘ of movies coming from comic books.

The followings ↘ are a few recent examples of comics turned‿into movies: /

Blade / Hellboy / Hulk / The mask / Men in black

Step ❸

 # Read Slowly

스스로 끊어 읽기와 억양을 직접 표시하면서,
천천히 큰 소리로 읽어 보세요.

1회 □ 2회 □ 3회 □ 4회 □ 5회 □ 6회 □ 7회 □

It's not uncommon for movies to come from comic books.

You might know some famous examples like *Spiderman*, *Superman*, and *X-Men*.

There are many other cases of movies coming from comic books.

The followings are a few recent examples of comics turned into movies:

Blade Hellboy Hulk The mask Men in black

Step ❹

Read Normal Speed with shadowing

자신이 생겼다면 이제 내용을 전달하면서 큰 소리로 따라 읽어 보세요.

1회 □   2회 □   3회 □   4회 □   5회 □   6회 □   7회 □

Step ❺

Speak / Presentation

이제는 아래 글을 완성하면서 큰 소리로 사람들 앞에서 발표해 보세요.

It's not uncommon for movies to _____ _____ _____ _____. You might know _____ _____ _____ like *Spiderman*, *Superman*, and *X-Men*. There are many other _____ ___ _____ _____ from comic books. ____ _____ ____ __ few recent examples of comics turned into movies:

Blade   Hellboy   Hulk   The mask   Men in black

> ### ○ Script
>
> 만화책에서 영화가 탄생하는 것은 일반적인 일이다. 아마 여러분도 "스파이더맨", "슈퍼맨", 그리고 "엑스맨" 같은 몇 가지 유명한 예를 알고 있을 것이다. 그 외에도 만화책을 바탕으로 한 영화는 무척 많다. 다음의 예들은 최근에 영화로 탈바꿈한 만화들이다. "블레이드" "헬보이" "헐크" "마스크" "맨 인 블랙"
>
> - 정답 > **d. Movies that came from comic books**

Take a break

▶ 영어발음을 향상시키는 방법

th를 발음해 보세요!

th 발음을 어떻게 하는지 아시죠? 가끔은 제대로 발음을 할 수도 있지만 급하게 발음할 때는 긴장을 해서 잘못 발음하는 경우가 있습니다. 보통 s 발음을 하게 됩니다. 예를 들어 three를 [s-ree]라고 하거나 something을 [썸씽]이라고 발음을 하는 경우가 종종 있습니다. 혓바닥 끝을 살짝 물면서 힘을 주어 발음해 보세요.

Topic 11 LEVEL 1

JOIN THE GIRL SCOUTS NOW!

지금, 걸 스카우트에 참여하자!

Step ❶

Understanding

음원을 들으면서 눈으로 읽어 보고,
문제를 통해서 이해했는지 확인해 보세요.

Founded in 1912, the Girl Scouts is an important American group. Today, there are nearly four million Girl Scouts; 2.8 million members (ages of 5 to 17) and 986,000 adult volunteers in total. Girl Scouts learn many skills, from cooking to fixing computers. These skills are really useful and invaluable later in life for all the girls.

 윗글의 내용과 일치하는 것은?

ⓐ The Girl Scouts was founded in 1910.
ⓑ The Girl Scouts isn't an important American group.
ⓒ 5 to 17-year-old girls can be members of the Girl Scouts.
ⓓ There are four million adult volunteers for the Girl Scouts.

 ▪ found 창설되다, 창립되다

Step ❷

Listening

이번에는 억양과 끊어 읽기, 연음과 강조어에 대한 강의를 들어 보세요.

/ 끊어 읽기   ∫↘ 억양   볼드색 강세를 두어 읽는 부분   ⌣ 연음

Founded in 1912, / the Girl Scouts is an ↘important American group.

Today, / there are **nearly** four million Girl Scouts; / 2.8 million members / (ages of 5 to 17) / **and** 986,000 adult volunteers in total.

Girl Scouts learn **many** skills, / from cooking‿to fixing computers.

These skills are ∫really useful and / invaluable later in ↘ life for all‿the girls.

Step ❸

Read Slowly

스스로 끊어 읽기와 억양을 직접 표시하면서,
천천히 큰 소리로 읽어 보세요.

1회 ☐ 2회 ☐ 3회 ☐ 4회 ☐ 5회 ☐ 6회 ☐ 7회 ☐

Founded in 1912, the Girl Scouts is an important American group.

Today, there are nearly four million Girl Scouts; 2.8 million members (ages of 5 to 17) and 986,000 adult volunteers in total.

Girl Scouts learn many skills, from cooking to fixing computers.

These skills are really useful and invaluable later in life for all the girls.

Step ❹

Read Normal Speed with shadowing
자신이 생겼다면 이제 내용을 전달하면서 큰 소리로 따라 읽어 보세요.

1회 □   2회 □   3회 □   4회 □   5회 □   6회 □   7회 □

Step ❺

Speak / Presentation
이제는 아래 글을 완성하면서 큰 소리로 사람들 앞에서 발표해 보세요.

Founded in 1912, the Girl Scouts ____ ____ _____ American group. Today, there ____ _____ ____ _____ Girl Scouts; 2.8 million members (ages of 5 to 17) and 986,000 adult volunteers in total. Girl Scouts _____ _____ _____, from cooking to fixing computers. These skills are really useful and invaluable _____ ___ _____ _____ _____ the girls.

○ Script

1912년 창립된 걸 스카웃(Girl Scouts)은 미국의 중요한 단체이다. 오늘날, 걸 스카웃은 거의 4백만 명에 달하는데, 그 중 단원(5세부터 17세)이 280만 명이고, 성인 자원 봉사자가 98만 6천 명이다. 걸 스카웃은 요리부터 시작해서 컴퓨터 수리에 이르기까지 많은 기술들을 배운다. 이런 기술들은 훗날 많은 소녀들에게 아주 유용하고 가치 있게 사용된다.

- 정답 > c. 5 to 17-year-old girls can be members of the Girl Scouts.

Take a break

▶ 영어발음을 향상시키는 방법

z와 s를 발음해 보세요!

동물원이 영어로 뭐죠? 네, zoo입니다. 앗! 혹시 방금 [주]라고 발음하셨나요? 그럼 zebra를 발음해 보세요. 혹시 [집라]라고 하셨나요? 기억하세요! z 발음을 할 때 j 발음을 하시면 안 됩니다! s 발음을 할 때처럼 윗니와 아랫니를 살짝 대면서 혀를 이빨 뒤에 놓고 진동하듯이 발음하면 됩니다. 그러나, s 발음이 나면 안 되죠. 다시 한 번 한국식 발음이 들리지 않도록 연습해 보세요!

Topic 12 LEVEL 1

MIDDLE SCHOOL ENTRANCE EXAM CHANGES

중학교 입학시험 제도의 변화

Step ❶

Understanding

음원을 들으면서 눈으로 읽어 보고,
문제를 통해서 이해했는지 확인해 보세요.

In the past, students used to take an entrance exam for middle school. They took it after finishing elementary school. This changed in 1969. Since then, students don't take an entrance exam for middle school. They just go to middle schools close to their home, usually. Most students like this system better. Now they don't have to take an exam!

윗글의 내용과 일치하지 않는 것은?
ⓐ Many students like today's middle school entrance system.
ⓑ Today, students usually go to middle schools close to their home.
ⓒ The entrance system changed in 1969.
ⓓ Students don't study hard in middle school.

- used to ~하곤 했다
- elementary school 초등학교

Step ❷

Listening

이번에는 억양과 끊어 읽기, 연음과 강조어에 대한 강의를 들어 보세요.

/ 끊어 읽기   ↗ ↘ 억양   **볼드색** 강세를 두어 읽는 부분   ‿ 연음

In the past, / students used‿to take an ↗entrance exam for middle school.

They took‿it after finishing elementary school.

This changed ↘ in 1969.

Since then, / students don't take an entrance exam for ↘ middle school.

They just go to middle schools close to their ↘ home, / usually.

↗**Most** students like this system ↘ better.

Now / they **don't** have‿to take an exam! ↗

Step ❸

Read Slowly

스스로 끊어 읽기와 억양을 직접 표시하면서,
천천히 큰 소리로 읽어 보세요.

1회 □ 2회 □ 3회 □ 4회 □ 5회 □ 6회 □ 7회 □

In the past, students used to take an entrance exam for middle school.

They took it after finishing elementary school.

This changed in 1969.

Since then, students don't take an entrance exam for middle school.

They just go to middle schools close to their home, usually.

Most students like this system better.

Now they don't have to take an exam!

Step ④

Read Normal Speed with shadowing

자신이 생겼다면 이제 내용을 전달하면서 큰 소리로 따라 읽어 보세요.

1회 □   2회 □   3회 □   4회 □   5회 □   6회 □   7회 □

Step ⑤

Speak / Presentation

이제는 아래 글을 완성하면서 큰 소리로 사람들 앞에서 발표해 보세요.

In the past, _____ ____ ___ _____ an entrance exam for middle school. They took it after finishing elementary school. _____ _____ in 1969. Since then, students don't _____ ___ _____ _____ for middle school. _____ _____ ___ ___ middle schools close to their home, usually. Most students like this _____ _____. Now _____ _____ _____ ___ take an exam!

○ Script

과거에 학생들은 중학교 입학시험을 치렀다. 이들은 초등학교를 졸업하고 시험을 봤다. 1969년에 이 제도가 바뀌어, 그 이후로는 학생들이 중학교 입학시험을 치르지 않는다. 보통 그들은 집에서 가까운 중학교로 가기만 하면 된다. 대부분의 학생들은 이 시스템을 더 좋아한다. 이제 그들은 시험을 칠 필요가 없다.

● 정답 > d. Students don't study hard in middle school.

Take a break

▶ 영어발음을 향상시키는 방법

drink를 발음해 보세요!

drink를 한 번 읽어 보세요. 지금 d와 r을 따로 발음하셨나요? 그렇게 하셨다면 잘못된 발음입니다! dr은 항상 한 번에 함께 발음을 해야 합니다. 그리고 더 놀라운 것은 [jr]처럼 발음이 나와야 한다는 것입니다. 예를 들어, drink는 [jrink]로 들린다는 거죠. dr로 시작하는 모든 단어들이 이런 소리를 만들 수 있도록 해야 합니다.

Topic 13

LEVEL 1

THE FORMATION OF N SYNC

'엔 씽크' 뮤직 밴드의 형성

Step ❶

Understanding

음원을 들으면서 눈으로 읽어 보고,
문제를 통해서 이해했는지 확인해 보세요.

In 1996, five special young men made a band together. Then, they made a CD. Soon after that, they changed the world. That's the short history about the group known as N sync. Five young men from different parts of the United States met in Orlando, Florida and created a very successful music group. The name N sync comes from the first names of the band members: JustiN, ChriS, JoeY, LansteN, and JC.

 윗글의 주제로 알맞은 것은?
ⓐ The history of N sync
ⓑ The American pop singer
ⓒ Famous young men
ⓓ The music of Florida

 ▪ first name 이름

Step ❷

Listening

이번에는 억양과 끊어 읽기, 연음과 강조어에 대한
강의를 들어 보세요.

/ 끊어 읽기   ↗↘ 억양   **볼드색 강세를 두어 읽는 부분**   ‿ 연음

In 1996, / five special young men / made a band together.

Then, / **they** made a CD.

Soon after that / they changed the world.

That's the short ↘ history about the group known as N sync.

Five young men from different parts of the United States /

met‿in Orlando, / Florida and ↗ created a very successful

music group.

The name N sync comes‿from the ↗ first names of the band

members: / JustiN, / ChriS, / JoeY, / LansteN, / and JC.

Step ❸

Read Slowly

스스로 끊어 읽기와 억양을 직접 표시하면서,
천천히 큰 소리로 읽어 보세요.

1회 □ 2회 □ 3회 □ 4회 □ 5회 □ 6회 □ 7회 □

In 1996, five special young men made a band together.

Then, they made a CD.

Soon after that, they changed the world.

That's the short history about the group known as N sync.

Five young men from different parts of the United States met in Orlando, Florida and created a very successful music group.

The name N sync comes from the first names of the band members: JustiN, ChriS, JoeY, LansteN, and JC.

Step ❹

Read Normal Speed with shadowing
자신이 생겼다면 이제 내용을 전달하면서 큰 소리로 따라 읽어 보세요.

1회 □   2회 □   3회 □   4회 □   5회 □   6회 □   7회 □

Step ❺

Speak / Presentation
이제는 아래 글을 완성하면서 큰 소리로 사람들 앞에서 발표해 보세요.

In 1996, five special young _____ _____ ___ _____ together. _____, _____ made a CD. Soon after that, they _____ ____ _____. That's _____ _____ _____ _____ the group known as N sync. _____ _____ ___ _____ different parts of the United States met in Orlando, Florida and created a very successful music group. The name N sync _____ _____ ____ _____ names of the band members: JustiN, ChriS, JoeY, LansteN, and JC.

○ Script

1996년, 5명의 특별한 젊은이들이 모여 밴드를 결성하고, CD를 만들었다. 그리고 얼마 후 그들은 세계를 바꾸었다. 이것이 '엔 싱크'라는 그룹에 관한 짧은 역사이다. 다섯 명의 젊은이들은 미국의 각기 다른 주 출신으로 플로리다 주 올란도에서 만났고, 아주 성공적인 음악 그룹을 탄생시켰다. '엔 싱크'라는 이름은 각 멤버의 이름에서 따온 것이다. 저스틴(JunsiN)의 N, 크리스(ChriS)의 S, 조이(JoeY)의 Y, 랜스턴(LansteN)의 N, 그리고 JC의 C, 이렇게 하여 '엔 싱크(N sync)'가 되었다.

- 정답 > a. The history of N sync

Take a break

▶ 영어발음을 향상시키는 방법

girl을 발음해 보세요!

어떤 단어들은 글자들을 서로 연결해서 자연스러운 발음이 나와야 합니다. 예를 들어, girl을 발음해 보세요. 많은 한국인들은 -irl 소리를 혀를 굴리면서 하는 것을 힘들어 합니다. 이때는 위와 아랫입술을 중간으로 모으면서 [er] 소리를 만들어야 합니다. 혀도 중간으로 살짝 뭉쳐지죠! r 발음을 굴리면 약간 어색하다고 느낄 수도 있지만 좀 더 연습하면 더 자연스럽게 될 것입니다.

Topic 14

LEVEL 1

STAY AWAY FROM SODA POP!

소다수 음료를 멀리 하자!

Step ❶

Understanding

음원을 들으면서 눈으로 읽어 보고,
문제를 통해서 이해했는지 확인해 보세요.

Many young people love soft drinks, or soda pop. In the United States, more than 30 percent of teenagers drink at least three cans of soda pop a day. Soda pop may taste good but it can have very bad side effects on your health, especially for children and teenagers. Did you know, for example, that drinking too much soda pop can lead to obesity, caffeine dependence, tooth decay, and weakened bones?

윗글의 내용과 일치하지 않는 것은?

ⓐ Soda pop is popular among teenagers.
ⓑ Drinking soda pop is healthy for children and teenagers.
ⓒ Soda pop can have bad side effects on people's health.
ⓓ Almost one-third of teenagers in America drink at least three cans of soda pop a day.

Voca.
- soda pop 소다수
- obesity 비만
- tooth decay 충치
- caffeine dependence 카페인 의존증

Step ❷

Listening

이번에는 억양과 끊어 읽기, 연음과 강조어에 대한
강의를 들어 보세요.

/ 끊어 읽기   ↗↘ 억양   **볼드색** 강세를 두어 읽는 부분   ‿ 연음

Many young people love soft drinks, / or soda pop.

In‿the United States, / more than ↗30 percent of teenagers drink at least three cans↘ of soda pop a day.

Soda pop may taste good / but it can have **very** bad side effects↘ on your health, / **especially** for ↗children / and teenagers.

Did you know, / for example, / that drinking too‿much soda pop can lead to obesity, / caffeine dependence, / tooth decay, / and weakened bones? ↗

Step ❸

 **Read Slowly**

스스로 끊어 읽기와 억양을 직접 표시하면서,
천천히 큰 소리로 읽어 보세요.

1회 □   2회 □   3회 □   4회 □   5회 □   6회 □   7회 □

Many young people love soft drinks, or soda pop.

In the United States, more than 30 percent of teenagers drink at least three cans of soda pop a day.

Soda pop may taste good but it can have very bad side effects on your health, especially for children and teenagers.

Did you know, for example, that drinking too much soda pop can lead to obesity, caffeine dependence, tooth decay, and weakened bones?

Step ❹

Read Normal Speed with shadowing
자신이 생겼다면 이제 내용을 전달하면서 큰 소리로 따라 읽어 보세요.

1회 □   2회 □   3회 □   4회 □   5회 □   6회 □   7회 □

Step ❺

Speak / Presentation
이제는 아래 글을 완성하면서 큰 소리로 사람들 앞에서 발표해 보세요.

Many young people love soft drinks, ____ ____ ____. In the United States, more than 30 percent of teenagers ____ ____ ____ ____ ____ of soda pop a day. Soda ____ ____ ____ ____ but it can have very bad side effects on your health, especially for children and teenagers. Did you know, for example, that drinking too much soda pop ____ ____ ___ ____, caffeine dependence, tooth decay, and weakened bones?

○ Script

많은 젊은이들은 소프트 드링크, 또는 소다수라고 불리는 탄산음료를 좋아한다. 미국 십대 중 30퍼센트 정도가 하루에 탄산음료를 적어도 3캔은 마신다. 탄산음료가 맛있을지는 모르지만 사람들, 특히 어린이와 십대들의 건강에 아주 나쁜 부작용을 일으킬 수 있다. 그 예로, 지나친 탄산음료 섭취가 비만, 카페인 중독, 충치, 그리고 뼈를 약화시킨다는 사실을 알고 있는가?

- 정답 > b. Drinking soda pop is healthy for children and teenagers.

Take a break

▶ 영어발음을 향상시키는 방법

Pick up the phone!을 말해 보세요!

혹시 phone을 발음하셨을 때 f 대신에 p 발음으로 하셨나요? 여기서 ph는 꼭 f 발음으로 하도록 항상 주의하세요. 물론 연습을 많이 해야 합니다. 이렇게 발음을 하지 않으면 완전히 다른 단어로 들릴 수가 있습니다.

Topic 15 LEVEL 1

A FANTASY CAN BECOME A REALITY

공상 소설이 현실로 되다

Step ❶

Understanding

음원을 들으면서 눈으로 읽어 보고,
문제를 통해서 이해했는지 확인해 보세요.

Science fiction is not always just a story. In the past, some things happened only in books. Now, sometimes they also happen in real life. For example, in the past you could not get a new heart or liver. Now you can. In the past there were no robot dogs, but now there are. They are not soft like a real puppy, but they bark and walk around. Science fiction writers sometimes write about flying cars. We do not have flying cars now, but who knows? Maybe we will soon.

 윗글의 주제로 알맞은 것은?
ⓐ A story about science
ⓑ Science fiction stories happening in real life
ⓒ Getting a new heart, a liver, and robot dogs
ⓓ Writing a science fiction story about flying cars

Voca.   • science fiction 공상 과학 소설

Step ❷

Listening

이번에는 억양과 끊어 읽기, 연음과 강조어에 대한 강의를 들어 보세요.

/ 끊어 읽기　↗↘ 억양　**볼드색** 강세를 두어 읽는 부분　‿ 연음

Science fiction is **not** always ↘ just a story.

In the past, / some things happened only‿in books.

Now, / sometimes they ↗ also happen in real life.

For example, / in the past / you could not ↗ get a new heart or liver.

Now you can.

In the past / there were no robot dogs, / but now ↗ there are.

They are not soft like‿a real puppy, / but they bark and ↘ walk around.

Science fiction writers sometimes ↗ write‿about flying cars.

We do not have flying cars now, / but who knows? ↗

Maybe we will soon.

Step ❸

Read Slowly

스스로 끊어 읽기와 억양을 직접 표시하면서,
천천히 큰 소리로 읽어 보세요.

1회 □   2회 □   3회 □   4회 □   5회 □   6회 □   7회 □

Science fiction is not always just a story.

In the past, some things happened only in books.

Now, sometimes they also happen in real life.

For example, in the past you could not get a new heart or liver.

Now you can.

In the past there were no robot dogs, but now there are.

They are not soft like a real puppy, but they bark and walk around.

Science fiction writers sometimes write about flying cars.

We do not have flying cars now, but who knows?

Maybe we will soon.

Step ④

Read Normal Speed with shadowing

자신이 생겼다면 이제 내용을 전달하면서 큰 소리로 따라 읽어 보세요.

1회 ☐ 2회 ☐ 3회 ☐ 4회 ☐ 5회 ☐ 6회 ☐ 7회 ☐

Step ⑤

Speak / Presentation

이제는 아래 글을 완성하면서 큰 소리로 사람들 앞에서 발표해 보세요.

Science fiction is not ____ ____ __ story. ____ ____ ____, some things happened only in books. Now, sometimes they also happen in real life. For example, in the past ____ ____ ___ ___ __ new heart or liver. Now you can. In the past there ____ ___ ____ ____, but now there are. They are ____ ____ ____ a real puppy, but they bark and walk around. Science fiction writers _____ ____ ___ flying cars. We do not have flying cars now, ____ ____ ____? Maybe ____ ____ soon.

○ Script

공상 과학 소설이 반드시 허무맹랑한 이야기로 그치는 것은 아니다. 과거에는 어떤 일들은 책에서만 가능했다. 그러나 지금은 그런 것들이 실생활에서도 벌어지고 있다. 예를 들면, 옛날에는 심장이나 간을 새로 이식할 수 없었다. 그러나 지금은 그렇게 할 수 있다. 과거에는 로봇 애완견이란 것이 없었지만 지금은 있다. 진짜 강아지처럼 부드럽지는 않지만 그래도 짖기도 하고 걸어 다닌다. 간혹 공상 과학 소설가들은 날아다니는 자동차에 관해서 글을 쓰기도 한다. 현재는 날아다니는 차가 없지만, 누가 알겠는가? 곧 그런 차가 등장할지도 모른다.

- **정답** > b. Science fiction stories happening in real life

Take a break

▶ 영어발음을 향상시키는 방법

people을 발음해 보세요!

이번에는 people을 한 번 발음해 보세요! 많은 한국인들은 -ple로 끝나는 단어들은 [플]이라고 발음을 합니다. 따라서 [피플]이라고 많이들 하죠. 하지만 이건 한국식 발음이고 [피쁠]이 더 맞습니다. 끝부분에는 p 발음보다 [쁘]의 소리가 납니다. 예를 들어, sample에서도 p 소리는 들리지 않고 [sam-쁘-le]이라고 하죠. 좀 어색할 수도 있지만 이렇게 연습을 하시면 더 자연스러운 발음이 됩니다.

READ ALOUD

LEVEL 2

LEVEL 2

Topic no.	Title
01	Walt Disney Will Bring Joy Into Our Lives Forever
02	Be Aware Of The Global Warming!
03	Fight Off The Cold
04	Decorate My Pasta!
05	The Best Ways To Make The Best Jack-O'-Lantern
06	Save The Koala Bears
07	Volleyball On The Sand
08	The Rising Popularity Of The Japanese Animated Films
09	The True Football Fans Exist In America
10	Craving For A Hot Dog?
11	Students Want To Show Their Own Styles
12	Vegetables Are Good For Cars Too!
13	The Olympic Games Will Be Treasured Forever
14	Fly Up In A Hot Air Balloon
15	Flying Mammals

Topic 01

LEVEL 2

WALT DISNEY WILL BRING JOY INTO OUR LIVES FOREVER

월트 디즈니는 우리의 삶 속에 기쁨을 영원히 가져다줄 것이다

Step ❶

Understanding

음원을 들으면서 눈으로 읽어 보고,
문제를 통해서 이해했는지 확인해 보세요.

Walt Disney, the creator of Mickey Mouse and the founder of the Walt Disney Company, was born in Chicago in 1901. In 1928 he created the world-famous character, Mickey Mouse. After that, he made lots of wonderful characters like Donald Duck, Snow White, and Pinocchio. In 1955, he built the first Disneyland Park and got all the Disney characters together. Disney died in 1966, but the Walt Disney company is still making movies with his characters. Last year the company made *Finding Nemo*. Walt Disney is no longer here, but he will always bring joy and happiness to all of us.

 윗글의 전개 방식으로 알맞은 것은?
ⓐ Time order
ⓑ Alphabetical order
ⓒ Numerical order
ⓓ Age order

- create 만들다
- Snow White 백설 공주

Step ❷

Listening

이번에는 억양과 끊어 읽기, 연음과 강조어에 대한
강의를 들어 보세요.

/ 끊어 읽기   ∫ ↘ 억양   **볼드색** 강세를 두어 읽는 부분   ‿ 연음

Walt Disney, / the creator ∫ of Mickey Mouse and the founder of
the Walt Disney Company, / was‿born in Chicago in 1901.
In 1928 / he created the **world-famous** character, / Mickey
Mouse.
After that, / he made lots‿of wonderful characters / like ↘ Donald
Duck, / Snow White, / **and** Pinocchio.
In 1955, / he built the first ∫ Disneyland Park and got all‿the
Disney characters together.
Disney died in 1966, / but the Walt Disney company is still ↘
making movies with his characters.
Last year / the company made Finding Nemo.
Walt Disney is‿no longer here, / but he will always ∫ bring joy
and happiness to all of‿us.

Step ❸

Read Slowly

스스로 끊어 읽기와 억양을 직접 표시하면서,
천천히 큰 소리로 읽어 보세요.

1회 □ 2회 □ 3회 □ 4회 □ 5회 □ 6회 □ 7회 □

Walt Disney, the creator of Mickey Mouse and the founder of the Walt Disney Company, was born in Chicago in 1901.

In 1928 he created the world-famous character, Mickey Mouse.

After that, he made lots of wonderful characters like Donald Duck, Snow White, and Pinocchio.

In 1955, he built the first Disneyland Park and got all the Disney characters together.

Disney died in 1966, but the Walt Disney company is still making movies with his characters.

Last year the company made *Finding Nemo*.

Walt Disney is no longer here, but he will always bring joy and happiness to all of us.

Step ❹

Read Normal Speed with shadowing
자신이 생겼다면 이제 내용을 전달하면서 큰 소리로 따라 읽어 보세요.

1회 ☐ 2회 ☐ 3회 ☐ 4회 ☐ 5회 ☐ 6회 ☐ 7회 ☐

Step ❺

Speak / Presentation
이제는 아래 글을 완성하면서 큰 소리로 사람들 앞에서 발표해 보세요.

Walt Disney, ___ ____ __ Mickey Mouse and the founder of the Walt Disney Company, was born in Chicago in 1901. In 1928 ___ _____ ___ world-famous character, Mickey Mouse. After that, he made ____ __ _____ _____ like Donald Duck, Snow White, and Pinocchio. In 1955, he _____ ___ ____ Disneyland Park and got all the Disney characters together. Disney died in 1966, but the Walt Disney company ___ ____ _____ _____ with his characters. ____ ____ __ company made *Finding Nemo*. Walt Disney ___ __ _____ ____, but he will always bring joy and happiness to all of us.

○ Script

미키 마우스를 창조한 사람이자 월트 디즈니 회사의 창설자인 월트 디즈니는 1901년에 시카고에서 태어났다. 1928년에 그는 세계적으로 유명한 만화 주인공인 미키 마우스를 창조했다. 그 이후 월트 디즈니는 도널드 덕, 백설 공주, 피노키오 같은 멋진 주인공들을 많이 만들어 냈다. 1955년에 그는 최초의 디즈니랜드 공원을 지어, 디즈니 주인공들을 모두 한데 모았다. 디즈니는 1966년에 죽었지만 월트 디즈니 사는 여전히 이들 캐릭터를 이용한 영화를 만들고 있다. 작년에는 "니모를 찾아서"를 제작했다. 월트 디즈니는 이제 이 세상 사람이 아니지만 앞으로도 우리에게 기쁨과 행복을 안겨 줄 것이다.

- 정답 > a. Time order

Take a break

▶ 영어발음을 향상시키는 방법

door를 발음해 보세요!

door라는 단어는 발음하기가 쉽다고 생각하시죠? 하지만 이런 단어도 가끔 잘못 발음하는 분들이 있습니다. door에서 -oor를 [우r]라고 발음한다고 생각하면 안 됩니다! 이 발음은 항상 or를 발음할 때처럼 하셔야 됩니다. 그리고 r 발음을 끝부분에서 잘 마무리 하셔야 합니다. roar도 이 발음과 동일한 경우입니다.

Topic 02

LEVEL 2

BE AWARE OF THE GLOBAL WARMING!

지구온난화를 경계하라!

Step ❶

Understanding

음원을 들으면서 눈으로 읽어 보고,
문제를 통해서 이해했는지 확인해 보세요.

What is global warming? Global warming is just what it says an increase in the temperature of the air around the earth. Over a long time, it causes changes in weather patterns. A study published in 2003 by The Korea Environment Institute said that in one hundred years global warming will raise the sea level by 1 meter. This will flood some of Korea, causing loss of life and property.

 지구온난화가 원인이 되는 것은?

ⓐ It creates an unclean atmosphere.
ⓑ It causes changes in weather patterns.
ⓒ It causes the weather patterns to become stable.
ⓓ It makes the temperature go down.

 ▪ publish 출판하다   ▪ property 재산

Step ❷

Listening

이번에는 억양과 끊어 읽기, 연음과 강조어에 대한
강의를 들어 보세요.

/ 끊어 읽기   ∫↙ 억양   **볼드색 강세를 두어 읽는 부분**   ‿ 연음

What ∫ is global warming? ↙
Global warming is **just** what it says / an increase in the temperature of‿the air around ↙ the earth.
Over‿a long time, / it causes changes ↙ in weather patterns.
A study published in 2003 by The Korea Environment Institute said that / in one hundred years / global warming will raise the sea level by 1 meter.
This will flood some of Korea, / causing loss ∫ of life and property.

Step ❸

Read Slowly

스스로 끊어 읽기와 억양을 직접 표시하면서,
천천히 큰 소리로 읽어 보세요.

1회 □ 2회 □ 3회 □ 4회 □ 5회 □ 6회 □ 7회 □

What is global warming?

Global warming is just what it says an increase in the temperature of the air around the earth.

Over a long time, it causes changes in weather patterns.

A study published in 2003 by The Korea Environment Institute said that in one hundred years global warming will raise the sea level by 1 meter.

This will flood some of Korea, causing loss of life and property.

Step ❹

Read Normal Speed with shadowing
자신이 생겼다면 이제 내용을 전달하면서 큰 소리로 따라 읽어 보세요.

1회 □ 2회 □ 3회 □ 4회 □ 5회 □ 6회 □ 7회 □

Step ❺

Speak / Presentation
이제는 아래 글을 완성하면서 큰 소리로 사람들 앞에서 발표해 보세요.

What is _____ _____? Global warming is just what it says an increase in the _____ ____ ____ ____ around the earth. ____ ____ ____ ____, it causes changes in weather patterns. A _____ _____ ____ 2003 by The Korea Environment Institute said that in one hundred years global warming will raise the sea level by 1 meter. This will flood some of Korea, _____ _____ ____ _____ and property.

○ Script

지구온난화란 무엇인가? 지구온난화란 문자 그대로 지구를 둘러싼 대기의 기온이 올라가는 것을 뜻한다. 이 현상은 장기간에 걸쳐 날씨의 유형을 변화시킨다. 2003년에 펴낸 한국환경정책평가연구원의 보고서에 의하면 백 년 후에는 지구온난화 현상으로 해수면이 1미터까지 상승한다고 한다. 이렇게 되면 한국의 일부도 물에 잠겨 인간의 생명과 재산에 손실이 초래될 것이다.

● 정답 > b. It causes changes in weather patterns.

Take a break

▶ 영어발음을 향상시키는 방법

show를 한번 발음해 보세요!

혹시 [쇼]라고 한국식으로 발음을 하셨나요? 그렇다면 발음을 교정하셔야 합니다! ow 발음은 정확히 o 글자를 발음하듯이 좀 길게 발음해야 됩니다. 위아래 입술이 동그랗게 모아진 상태에서, 소리를 내야 합니다. snow도 한번 똑같이 발음해 보세요. 끝 부분을 살짝 길게 늘려서 발음해야 합니다.

Topic 03

LEVEL 2

FIGHT OFF THE COLD

추위를 이겨내자

Step ❶

Understanding

음원을 들으면서 눈으로 읽어 보고,
문제를 통해서 이해했는지 확인해 보세요.

When winter comes, it's easy to catch a cold. There are several things you can do to keep yourself from catching a cold. One is eating a lot of fresh vegetables and fruit. Don't eat too much junk food. Another is getting regular exercise. Try to exercise even when it is cold. Next, stay away from your friends when they are coughing or sneezing. Also, always wash your hands after you have been outside. Last, you can get a flu shot, too. Try to do all these things to keep yourself healthy.

 윗글의 구성 방식으로 알맞은 것은?
ⓐ Sequence
ⓑ Listing
ⓒ Cause & Effect
ⓓ Comparison & Contrast

 • coughing 기침 • sneezing 재채기

Step ❷

Listening

이번에는 억양과 끊어 읽기, 연음과 강조어에 대한 강의를 들어 보세요.

/ 끊어 읽기   ↗↘ 억양   **볼드색** 강세를 두어 읽는 부분   ‿ 연음

When winter comes, / it's easy to catch ↘ a cold.
There are **several** things you can do / to keep yourself from‿catching a cold.
One / is eating a lot‿of fresh vegetables and ↗ fruit.
Don't eat **too** much junk food.
Another ↗ is getting regular exercise.
Try‿to exercise **even** when it is cold.
Next, / stay away from your friends / when they are coughing ↗ or sneezing.
Also, / **always** wash your hands / after you have ↘ been outside.
Last, / you can get a flu shot, / too.
Try to do all‿these things / to keep yourself healthy.

Step ❸

Read Slowly

스스로 끊어 읽기와 억양을 직접 표시하면서,
천천히 큰 소리로 읽어 보세요.

1회 □ 2회 □ 3회 □ 4회 □ 5회 □ 6회 □ 7회 □

When winter comes, it's easy to catch a cold.

There are several things you can do to keep yourself from catching a cold.

One is eating a lot of fresh vegetables and fruit.

Don't eat too much junk food.

Another is getting regular exercise.

Try to exercise even when it is cold.

Next, stay away from your friends when they are coughing or sneezing.

Also, always wash your hands after you have been outside.

Last, you can get a flu shot, too.

Try to do all these things to keep yourself healthy.

Step ❹

Read Normal Speed with shadowing

자신이 생겼다면 이제 내용을 전달하면서 큰 소리로 따라 읽어 보세요.

1회 ☐   2회 ☐   3회 ☐   4회 ☐   5회 ☐   6회 ☐   7회 ☐

Step ❺

Speak / Presentation

이제는 아래 글을 완성하면서 큰 소리로 사람들 앞에서 발표해 보세요.

When winter comes, it's easy ___ ___ ___ ___. There are _____ _____ ___ can do to keep yourself from catching a cold. ____ __ ___ a lot of fresh vegetables and fruit. Don't eat too ____ ____ ____. Another is _____ _____ exercise. ____ __ _____ even when it is cold. Next, ____ ____ from your friends when they are coughing or sneezing. Also, always ___ ___ ___ ___ you have been outside. Last, you ___ ___ a flu shot, too. Try to ___ ___ _____ things to keep yourself healthy.

○ Script

겨울이 오면 감기에 걸리기 쉽다. 그러나 감기를 멀리할 수 있는 여러 가지 방법이 있다. 그 중의 하나는 신선한 야채와 과일을 많이 먹는 것이다. 정크 푸드는 너무 많이 먹지 않도록 한다. 다른 하나는 규칙적으로 운동을 하는 것이다. 추워도 운동을 하도록 하자. 다음으로는 기침을 하거나 재채기를 하는 친구들과는 떨어져 있는 것이다. 또 언제나 밖에 나갔다 와서는 손을 씻자. 마지막으로, 독감 예방 주사를 맞도록 하자. 건강을 지키기 위해 이런 것들을 모두 해 보도록 하자.

● 정답 > b. Listing

Take a break

▶ 영어발음을 향상시키는 방법

full을 한번 발음해 보세요!

어떤 발음이 나올까요? 혹시 fool과 비슷하게 발음하셨나요? 그렇다면 틀리게 발음하신 것입니다. 많은 사람들이 이 단어를 발음할 때 u를 길게 소리 내는 [우] 소리처럼 말을 하는데, 사실은 입술을 옆으로 살짝 당기면서 [f-을]이라고 짧게 발음을 해야 합니다. 예를 들어, joyful과 colorful이란 단어들을 한번 연습해 보세요. 이렇게 꾸준히 연습을 하시면 발음 교정에 큰 도움이 될 것입니다.

Topic 04

LEVEL 2

DECORATE MY PASTA!

파스타를 장식하자!

Step ❶

Understanding

음원을 들으면서 눈으로 읽어 보고,
문제를 통해서 이해했는지 확인해 보세요.

There are many different kinds of pasta, not just spaghetti. One is the "Ribbon." This shape is about 3/4 centimeters wide and looks like a ribbon that you see on a present. Another is the "Tube." This shape is about 1 and 1/2 centimeters long and looks like a very little straw. One other is the "Bow." This shape is about 1 and a half centimeters long and looks like two triangles with the ends together. There are other shapes, too, but these are the most common.

 윗글의 내용으로 볼 때, 각각의 종류가 나열된 방식으로 알맞은 것은?

ⓐ The only important thing is at the end.
ⓑ The only important thing is at the beginning.
ⓒ Most important thing first to least important thing last.
ⓓ All things are equally important.

Voca.   • triangle 삼각형   • present 선물

Step ❷

Listening

이번에는 억양과 끊어 읽기, 연음과 강조어에 대한
강의를 들어 보세요.

/ 끊어 읽기   ∫ ⌡ 억양   **볼드색** 강세를 두어 읽는 부분   ⌣ 연음

There are many different kinds of pasta, / not ∫ just spaghetti.
One is‿the "Ribbon."
This shape ⌡ is about 3/4 centimeters wide / and looks like‿a
ribbon that you see on a ∫ present.
Another is the "Tube."
This shape is about ⌡ 1 and 1/2 centimeters long / and looks
like‿a **very** little straw.
One other / is the "Bow."
This shape is‿about / 1 and a half centimeters long / and **looks**
like two triangles ⌡ with‿the ends together.
There are other shapes, / too, / but these are the **most** common.

Step ❸

Read Slowly

스스로 끊어 읽기와 억양을 직접 표시하면서,
천천히 큰 소리로 읽어 보세요.

1회 □ 2회 □ 3회 □ 4회 □ 5회 □ 6회 □ 7회 □

There are many different kinds of pasta, not just spaghetti.

One is the "Ribbon."

This shape is about 3/4 centimeters wide and looks like a ribbon that you see on a present.

Another is the "Tube."

This shape is about 1 and 1/2 centimeters long and looks like a very little straw.

One other is the "Bow."

This shape is about 1 and a half centimeters long and looks like two triangles with the ends together.

There are other shapes, too, but these are the most common.

Step ④

Read Normal Speed with shadowing

자신이 생겼다면 이제 내용을 전달하면서 큰 소리로 따라 읽어 보세요.

1회 □ 2회 □ 3회 □ 4회 □ 5회 □ 6회 □ 7회 □

Step ⑤

Speak / Presentation

이제는 아래 글을 완성하면서 큰 소리로 사람들 앞에서 발표해 보세요.

There are many _____ ____ __ pasta, not just spaghetti. One is the "Ribbon." This shape is about 3/4 centimeters wide and looks ____ __ ____ ____ you see on a present. Another is the "Tube." This shape is about 1 and 1/2 centimeters long and looks like __ ____ ____ _____. One _____ ___ __ "Bow." This shape is about 1 and a half centimeters long and looks ____ ____ _____ ___ the ends together. There are other shapes, too, but these are ___ __ _____.

○ Script

파스타에는 스파게티만 있는 것이 아니라 종류가 아주 다양하다. 그 중의 하나는 '리본'이다. 이것은 폭이 3/4센티미터 정도로, 선물 포장에서 볼 수 있는 리본처럼 생겼다. 다른 하나는 '튜브'라고 하는데, 길이가 대략 1.5센티미터로, 아주 작은 빨대처럼 생겼다. 또 다른 것에는 '바우'가 있다. 이 형태는 길이가 1.5센티미터 정도로 삼각형 두 개의 끝을 붙여 놓은 것처럼 생겼다. 다른 모양도 있지만 이것들이 가장 흔하다.

- **정답** > d. All things are equally important.

Take a break

▶ 영어발음을 향상시키는 방법

book을 한번 발음해 보세요!

book이라는 단어는 발음하기가 비교적 쉽다고 생각하는 분들이 많을 것입니다. 하지만 많은 분들이 그냥 [북]이라고 -oo-를 길게 소리 내는 [우] 발음을 합니다. 그것은 정확한 영어발음이 아닙니다. 이것도 -ful과 비슷하게 입술을 옆으로 살짝 당기면서 짧게 [b-윽]이라고 중간에 끊지 말고 이어서 타이트하게 발음을 해야 합니다. took과 look도 이러한 방법으로 한번 연습해 보세요.

Topic 05

LEVEL 2

THE BEST WAYS TO MAKE THE BEST JACK-O'-LANTERN

최고의 호박등을 만드는 최상의 방법

Step ❶

Understanding

음원을 들으면서 눈으로 읽어 보고,
문제를 통해서 이해했는지 확인해 보세요.

Making a jack-o'-lantern for your Halloween party is easy. First, you have to cut out the top of a pumpkin. Next, take out the inside part with a large spoon. Choose a flat side of the pumpkin and draw a face on it. Then cut through the lines and push out the pieces. Last, put a candle on the inside. It is best to put the candle into a glass jar so that the wind won't blow it out. After you light the candle, turn off all the lights and watch the jack-o'-lantern smile.

Q! 윗글의 주제로 알맞은 것은?
ⓐ Halloween Party
ⓑ Cutting a pumpkin
ⓒ Making a jack-o'-lantern
ⓓ How to make a pumpkin

 Voca. • jack-o'-lantern 호박초롱, 호박등   • jar 단지

Step ❷

Listening

이번에는 억양과 끊어 읽기, 연음과 강조어에 대한 강의를 들어 보세요.

| / 끊어 읽기   ∫↘ 억양   **볼드색** 강세를 두어 읽는 부분   ‿ 연음 |

Making a jack-o'-lantern for your Halloween party ↘is easy.

First, / you have‿to cut out the top ∫ of a pumpkin.

Next, / take‿out the inside part with‿a **large** spoon.

Choose a flat side of the pumpkin / and draw a face on ↘it.

Then cut through the lines / and **push out** the pieces.

Last, / put‿a candle on‿the inside.

It is best ∫ to put the candle into‿a glass jar / so that the wind ↘ won't blow it out.

After you light the candle, / turn off **all the** lights and watch the jack-o'-lantern smile.

Step ❸

Read Slowly

스스로 끊어 읽기와 억양을 직접 표시하면서,
천천히 큰 소리로 읽어 보세요.

1회 □ 2회 □ 3회 □ 4회 □ 5회 □ 6회 □ 7회 □

Making a jack-o'-lantern for your Halloween party is easy.

First, you have to cut out the top of a pumpkin.

Next, take out the inside part with a large spoon.

Choose a flat side of the pumpkin and draw a face on it.

Then cut through the lines and push out the pieces.

Last, put a candle on the inside.

It is best to put the candle into a glass jar so that the wind won't blow it out.

After you light the candle, turn off all the lights and watch the jack-o'-lantern smile.

Step ④

Read Normal Speed with shadowing

자신이 생겼다면 이제 내용을 전달하면서 큰 소리로 따라 읽어 보세요.

1회 □ 2회 □ 3회 □ 4회 □ 5회 □ 6회 □ 7회 □

Step ⑤

Speak / Presentation

이제는 아래 글을 완성하면서 큰 소리로 사람들 앞에서 발표해 보세요.

Making a jack-o'-lantern for your Halloween ____ ___ ___. First, ____ ____ ___ ____ out the top of a pumpkin. Next, take out the inside part ____ ____ ____ ____. Choose ___ ____ ____ __ the pumpkin and draw a face on it. Then cut through the lines and ____ ____ ___ _____. Last, ____ ___ _____ ___ the inside. It is best to put the candle ____ __ _____ jar so that the wind won't blow it out. _____ ___ _____ ___ candle, turn off all the lights and watch the jack-o'-lantern smile.

○ Script

핼러윈 파티에 사용하는 호박등을 만드는 것은 쉽다. 먼저 호박의 맨 꼭대기를 잘라내야 한다. 다음에는 큰 숟가락으로 호박의 속을 파낸다. 그런 다음 호박의 평평한 면을 택해 얼굴을 그려 넣는다. 그리고는 줄을 따라 도려내고는 조각들을 밀어낸다. 마지막으로 속에다 양초를 넣으면 되는데, 바람이 불어도 촛불이 꺼지지 않도록 초는 유리로 된 단지 안에 넣는 것이 가장 좋다. 양초에 불을 붙인 후에 다른 불들은 모두 끄고, 호박등이 미소 짓는 모습을 보자.

- 정답 > c. Making a jack-o'-lantern

Take a break

▶ 영어발음을 향상시키는 방법

her라고 한번 발음해 보세요!

많은 분들이 [허-r]라고 어색한 발음을 합니다. -ir처럼 -er도 한국 사람들한테는 제대로 발음을 하기가 좀 어렵습니다. 이런 발음을 할 때에는 혀를 좀 더 굴리고 입술도 약간 오므린 상태로 발음해야 합니다. [허-r]라고 하지 말고, -er 발음을 더 타이트하게 들리는 소리를 내야 합니다. r 발음을 중점적으로 연습해 주세요!

Topic 06

LEVEL 2

SAVE THE KOALA BEARS

코알라를 보호하자

Step ❶

Understanding

음원을 들으면서 눈으로 읽어 보고,
문제를 통해서 이해했는지 확인해 보세요.

Koala bears are an *endangered species in Australia. One reason is that they are losing their homes and their food. Koalas live in eucalyptus trees. They eat only eucalyptus leaves. People are cutting down trees to make new buildings. The poor koala bears then have no place to live and cannot find enough food. Hunters are also a danger to koalas. They like to hunt koalas because their fur is soft and smooth. Nowadays there are laws to protect koalas. Anyone who hurts a koala is punished.

* endangered species - There are very few animals left in this group.

 윗글의 주제로 알맞은 것은?

ⓐ Why koala bears are endangered in Australia
ⓑ Why koala bears are dangerous to people
ⓒ Why koala bears can't find enough food
ⓓ Why koala bears aren't protected

Voca.   • fur 모피

Step ❷

Listening

이번에는 억양과 끊어 읽기, 연음과 강조어에 대한
강의를 들어 보세요.

/ 끊어 읽기   ∫ ↘ 억양   **볼드색 강세를 두어 읽는 부분**   ‿ 연음

Koala bears / are an endangered species in Australia.
One reason is that they are losing their homes and‿their food.
Koalas ∫ live in eucalyptus trees.
They eat only eucalyptus leaves.
People are cutting down trees to‿make new ↘ buildings.
The poor koala bears / then have no place to‿live / and
cannot ∫ find enough food.
Hunters are also a danger‿to ↘ koalas.
They like to hunt koalas / because their fur is soft **and** smooth.
Nowadays ∫ there are laws‿to protect koalas.
Anyone who hurts a koala / is punished.

Step ❸

Read Slowly

스스로 끊어 읽기와 억양을 직접 표시하면서,
천천히 큰 소리로 읽어 보세요.

1회 □ 2회 □ 3회 □ 4회 □ 5회 □ 6회 □ 7회 □

Koala bears are an endangered species in Australia.

One reason is that they are losing their homes and their food.

Koalas live in eucalyptus trees.

They eat only eucalyptus leaves.

People are cutting down trees to make new buildings.

The poor koala bears then have no place to live and cannot find enough food.

Hunters are also a danger to koalas.

They like to hunt koalas because their fur is soft and smooth.

Nowadays there are laws to protect koalas.

Anyone who hurts a koala is punished.

Step ❹

Read Normal Speed with shadowing

자신이 생겼다면 이제 내용을 전달하면서 큰 소리로 따라 읽어 보세요.

| 1회 ☐ | 2회 ☐ | 3회 ☐ | 4회 ☐ | 5회 ☐ | 6회 ☐ | 7회 ☐ |

Step ❺

Speak / Presentation

이제는 아래 글을 완성하면서 큰 소리로 사람들 앞에서 발표해 보세요.

___ ___ ___ an endangered species in Australia. One reason is that they are ___ ___ ___ ___ their food. Koalas live ___ ___ ___. ___ ___ only eucalyptus leaves. People are ___ ___ ___ ___ make new buildings. The poor koala bears then have no place to live and ___ ___ ___ food. Hunters are also ___ ___ ___ ___. They like to ___ ___ ___ their fur is soft and smooth. ___ ___ ___ ___ to protect koalas. Anyone who ___ ___ ___ ___ punished.

○ Script

코알라는 호주에서 멸종 위기*에 직면한 종이다. 서식지와 먹이를 빼앗기고 있는 것이 그 이유 중의 하나이다. 코알라는 유칼립투스 나무에서 살며, 유칼립투스 나뭇잎만 먹고 산다. 사람들이 새 건물을 짓느라 그 나무들을 베어 버리고 있다. 그래서 가엾은 코알라들은 살 곳이 없어지고 먹이를 제대로 찾아내지 못하게 되었다. 사냥꾼들도 코알라들을 위협하는 존재이다. 이 사람들은 코알라의 모피가 부드럽고 매끈하기 때문에 사냥하기를 좋아한다. 요즘에는 코알라를 보호하는 법이 생겼다. 따라서 코알라를 해치는 사람은 누구든지 처벌을 받는다.

* 멸종 위기의 종 – 이 종은 남아 있는 동물의 수가 극히 적다.

● 정답 > a. Why koala bears are endangered in Australia

Take a break

▶ 영어발음을 향상시키는 방법

for를 한번 발음해 보세요!

-or로 끝나는 단어들은 혀를 잘 굴릴 수가 없어서 발음하기가 좀 힘들 수 있습니다. 하지만 다른 발음들과 비슷하게 -or를 강조하면서 [오-r]라고 발음을 하시면 됩니다. 숫자 four를 발음할 때와 유사한 소리가 나면 됩니다. more도 한번 연습해 보세요.

Topic 07

LEVEL 2

VOLLEYBALL ON THE SAND

모래 위에서 하는 배구

Step ❶

Understanding

음원을 들으면서 눈으로 읽어 보고,
문제를 통해서 이해했는지 확인해 보세요.

Beach volleyball is an old sport, but it was not played in the Olympic Games until 1996. Beach volleyball was played for the first time on a beach in California in the early 1920s. For a long time, only people in California played beach volleyball. The sport became more popular year by year and by 1980 other states and countries played in the tournaments. The first beach volleyball Olympic event was in 1996 in Atlanta, Georgia (U.S.). There were 254 men's teams and 16 women's teams. Now many people think beach volleyball is one of the most fun events to watch. They say it is like a big beach party.

 윗글의 주제로 알맞은 것은?

ⓐ A story about beach
ⓑ The popular beach sport
ⓒ Beach volleyball has many rules.
ⓓ The first volleyball player in the U.S.

Voca. • states 주(州)

Step ❷

Listening

이번에는 억양과 끊어 읽기, 연음과 강조어에 대한 강의를 들어 보세요.

/ 끊어 읽기   ⌒ ⌣ 억양   볼드색 강세를 두어 읽는 부분   ‿ 연음

Beach volleyball ⌣is‿an old sport, / but it was **not** played in‿the Olympic Games until ⌒1996.
Beach volleyball was played for‿the first time / on a beach in California / in‿the early 1920s.
For a long time, /only ⌒people in California played beach volleyball.
The sport ⌣became more popular / year by year and‿by 1980 ⌒other states and countries played in‿the tournaments.
The first ⌒beach volleyball Olympic event / was in 1996 in Atlanta, / Georgia (U.S.).
There were ⌣254 men's teams / and 16 women's teams.
Now / many people think beach volleyball is one of the **most** fun events to ⌣watch.
They say ⌒it is like‿a **big** beach party.

Step ❸

Read Slowly

스스로 끊어 읽기와 억양을 직접 표시하면서,
천천히 큰 소리로 읽어 보세요.

1회 ☐ 2회 ☐ 3회 ☐ 4회 ☐ 5회 ☐ 6회 ☐ 7회 ☐

Beach volleyball is an old sport, but it was not played in the Olympic Games until 1996.

Beach volleyball was played for the first time on a beach in California in the early 1920s.

For a long time, only people in California played beach volleyball.

The sport became more popular year by year and by 1980 other states and countries played in the tournaments.

The first beach volleyball Olympic event was in 1996 in Atlanta, Georgia (U.S.).

There were 254 men's teams and 16 women's teams.

Now many people think beach volleyball is one of the most fun events to watch.

They say it is like a big beach party.

Step ❹

Read Normal Speed with shadowing
자신이 생겼다면 이제 내용을 전달하면서 큰 소리로 따라 읽어 보세요.

1회 □ 2회 □ 3회 □ 4회 □ 5회 □ 6회 □ 7회 □

Step ❺

Speak / Presentation
이제는 아래 글을 완성하면서 큰 소리로 사람들 앞에서 발표해 보세요.

Beach volleyball is an old sport, but ___ ___ ___ ___ in the Olympic Games until 1996. ___ ___ ___ ___ for the first time on a beach in California in the early 1920s. For a long time, ___ ___ ___ California played beach volleyball. The sport became more popular year by year and by 1980 other states and countries played ___ ___ ___. The ___ ___ ___ Olympic event was in 1996 in Atlanta, Georgia (U.S.). There were 254 men's ___ ___ 16 women's teams. Now many people think beach volleyball is one of the ___ ___ ___ ___ watch. ___ ___ ___ ___ like a big beach party.

○ Script

비치발리볼은 오래된 운동이지만 1996년에야 비로소 올림픽 경기가 되었다. 비치발리볼 경기는 1920년대 초에 캘리포니아 주 해변에서 처음 열렸다. 그 후 오랫동안 캘리포니아 사람들만 비치발리볼 경기를 했다. 그러나 해가 갈수록 이 운동은 인기를 얻게 되어, 1980년이 되자 다른 주와 나라에서도 이 경기를 토너먼트 형식으로 하게 되었다. 올림픽에서 비치발리볼이 경기로 채택된 것은 1996년에 미국의 조지아 주 애틀랜타 시에서 열린 것이 최초였다. 당시에는 남자 팀이 254개, 여자 팀이 16개 있었다. 이제는 많은 사람들이 비치발리볼을 가장 재미있게 볼 수 있는 경기 중의 하나라고 생각한다. 마치 대규모로 열리는 해변의 파티 같다고 사람들은 말한다.

● 정답 > b. The popular beach sport

Take a break

▶ 영어발음을 향상시키는 방법

open을 한번 발음해 보세요!

많은 한국인들은 이 단어의 정확한 발음을 배우게 되면 무척 놀랍니다. 첫 번째로 우선 [ㅍ] 발음을 내면 안 됩니다! 대신, [ㅃ] 소리를 내야 합니다. 그리고 -en을 [앤]이라고 하면 안 됩니다. 따라서 정확하게는 [o-쁜]이 됩니다. Open the door!를 한번 발음해 보세요! 여기에서 또다시 강조하고 싶은 것은 단어 뒤에 -en으로 끝날 때에는 [앤]이 아닌 -in 발음이 되어야 한다는 것입니다.

Topic 08   LEVEL 2

THE RISING POPULARITY OF THE JAPANESE ANIMATED FILMS

인기 폭등하고 있는 일본 만화 영화

Step ❶

Understanding

음원을 들으면서 눈으로 읽어 보고,
문제를 통해서 이해했는지 확인해 보세요.

Japanese animated films are different from American animated films. In Japan, there are animated films about almost any subject. There are many animated films for people of different ages. The films can be serious or silly. In the United States there are not many different types of animated films. Many people think of animation as short movies for small children. Animated films in the U.S. are not usually serious. Japanese animated films are popular in the United States now. There are many films with English subtitles or soundtracks.

윗글의 주제로 알맞은 것은?

ⓐ Japanese animated films
ⓑ Different types of animation in the United States
ⓒ Different types of Japanese animation
ⓓ Differences between Japanese animation and American animation

---

Voca. • silly 가벼운   • subtitle 자막

150

Step ❷

Listening

이번에는 억양과 끊어 읽기, 연음과 강조어에 대한
강의를 들어 보세요.

/ 끊어 읽기   ∫ ↘ 억양   **볼드색 강세를 두어 읽는 부분**   ‿ 연음

Japanese animated films are ↘different from American animated films.

In Japan, / there are animated ∫films about almost **any** subject.

There are many animated films for people‿of different ages.

The films can be serious / or silly.

In‿the United States / there are **not** many different types ↘of animated films.

Many ∫people think of animation / as short movies for ↘small children.

Animated films in‿the U.S. / are **not** usually serious.

Japanese animated films are popular in‿the United States now.

There are ↘many films / with English subtitles or soundtracks.

Step ❸

Read Slowly

스스로 끊어 읽기와 억양을 직접 표시하면서,
천천히 큰 소리로 읽어 보세요.

1회 □ 2회 □ 3회 □ 4회 □ 5회 □ 6회 □ 7회 □

Japanese animated films are different from American animated films.

In Japan, there are animated films about almost any subject.

There are many animated films for people of different ages.

The films can be serious or silly.

In the United States there are not many different types of animated films.

Many people think of animation as short movies for small children.

Animated films in the U.S. are not usually serious.

Japanese animated films are popular in the United States now.

There are many films with English subtitles or soundtracks.

Step ④

Read Normal Speed with shadowing
자신이 생겼다면 이제 내용을 전달하면서 큰 소리로 따라 읽어 보세요.

1회 □ 2회 □ 3회 □ 4회 □ 5회 □ 6회 □ 7회 □

Step ⑤

Speak / Presentation
이제는 아래 글을 완성하면서 큰 소리로 사람들 앞에서 발표해 보세요.

Japanese _____ ___ ___ _____ from American animated films. In Japan, there are animated films about _____ ___ _____. There are many animated films for _____ ___ _____ _____. The films can ___ _____ ___ _____. In the United States there are not ____ _____ ____ ___ animated films. Many people think of animation ___ ____ ____ ___ small children. Animated films in the U.S. are ___ _____ _____. Japanese animated _____ ___ _____ in the United States now. There are many films with English _____ ___ _____.

○ Script

일본의 만화 영화는 미국의 그것과는 다르다. 일본에는 거의 모든 주제에 대한 만화 영화가 있다. 또한 다양한 연령대의 만화 영화가 많이 있다. 진지한 것도 있고, 가벼운 것도 있다. 미국에서는 만화 영화 종류가 다양하지 않다. 만화 영화는 어린 아이들이 보는 짧은 영화라고 생각하는 사람들이 많다. 미국의 만화 영화는 보통 주제가 진지한 것은 아니다. 일본 만화 영화는 요즘 미국에서 인기를 얻고 있어서, 자막이나 사운드 트랙이 영어로 되어 있는 영화가 많다.

- 정답 > **d. Differences between Japanese animation and American animation**

Take a break

▶ 영어발음을 향상시키는 방법

contact를 한번 발음해 보세요!

[콘택트]와 비슷한 발음을 하셨나요? 많은 분들이 이 단어를 이렇게 잘못 발음합니다. con-으로 시작하는 단어들은 경우에 따라서 발음에 큰 차이가 있습니다. 어떤 경우에는 [칸]으로 발음해야 하고, 또 어떤 경우에는 [컨]으로 발음해야 할 때도 있습니다. 단어를 제대로 알고 많이 들어야만 자연스럽게 구별해서 발음할 수 있습니다. 위에 있는 단어는 [칸-tact]이고, control의 경우에는 [컨-트롤]입니다. 이와 같이 단어에 따라 발음이 달라지는 경우가 종종 있습니다.

Topic 09

LEVEL 2

THE TRUE FOOTBALL FANS EXIST IN AMERICA

진정한 미식축구 팬은 미국에 있다

Step ❶

Understanding

음원을 들으면서 눈으로 읽어 보고,
문제를 통해서 이해했는지 확인해 보세요.

American football fans sometimes seem crazy. They go to see their favorite teams play even in very bad weather. A big snowstorm or rainstorm cannot stop these crazy fans. Even in the snow you can see fans wearing the team colors and cheering wildly. It does not seem to matter if it snows a lot and they can't see anything clearly. American football fans seem to think that they have to be there. They seem to think that the players can't play well unless fans are there. Maybe they're right.

 윗글의 주제로 알맞은 것은?

ⓐ American football fans are not crazy about many sports.
ⓑ American football fans really enjoy watching football games.
ⓒ American football fans are getting tired of this sport.
ⓓ American football fans don't watch games when the weather is bad.

 ▪ snowstorm 눈보라   ▪ rainstorm 비바람, 폭풍우

Step ❷

Listening

이번에는 억양과 끊어 읽기, 연음과 강조어에 대한 강의를 들어 보세요.

/ 끊어 읽기   ∫ ↘ 억양   **볼드색 강세를 두어 읽는 부분**   ‿ 연음

American football fans / sometimes ∫ seem crazy.

They go‿to see their **favorite** teams play / even in very ∫ bad weather.

A big snowstorm / or rainstorm **cannot** stop these ↘ crazy fans.

Even in the snow / you can see fans wearing ↘ the‿team colors / and cheering wildly.

It does not ∫ seem to matter if it snows a lot / and they can't ∫ see anything clearly.

American football fans seem‿to think / that they **have** to‿be there.

They seem‿to think that the players can't play well / unless ∫ fans are there.

Maybe / they're right.

Step ❸

Read Slowly

스스로 끊어 읽기와 억양을 직접 표시하면서,
천천히 큰 소리로 읽어 보세요.

1회 ☐ 2회 ☐ 3회 ☐ 4회 ☐ 5회 ☐ 6회 ☐ 7회 ☐

American football fans sometimes seem crazy.

They go to see their favorite teams play even in very bad weather.

A big snowstorm or rainstorm cannot stop these crazy fans.

Even in the snow you can see fans wearing the team colors and cheering wildly.

It does not seem to matter if it snows a lot and they can't see anything clearly.

American football fans seem to think that they have to be there.

They seem to think that the players can't play well unless fans are there.

Maybe they're right.

Step ❹

Read Normal Speed with shadowing
자신이 생겼다면 이제 내용을 전달하면서 큰 소리로 따라 읽어 보세요.

1회 □   2회 □   3회 □   4회 □   5회 □   6회 □   7회 □

Step ❺

Speak / Presentation
이제는 아래 글을 완성하면서 큰 소리로 사람들 앞에서 발표해 보세요.

American football fans _____ _____ crazy. They go to see their favorite teams play _____ ___ _____ _____ weather. A big snowstorm ___ _____ _____ stop these crazy fans. Even in the snow you can see fans _____ ___ ___ ____ and cheering wildly. It ____ ___ ____ ___ matter if it snows a lot and they can't see anything clearly. _____ _____ ____ seem to think that they have to be there. They seem to think that the players ____ ___ ___ _____ fans are there. Maybe _____ _____.

○ Script

미식축구 팬들은 어떤 때는 광적으로 보이는 경우가 있다. 이 사람들은 날씨가 아무리 나빠도 자기들이 제일 좋아하는 팀의 경기를 보러 간다. 눈보라나 비바람이 몰아쳐도 이 열광적인 팬들을 막을 수는 없다. 눈을 맞으면서도 팀의 유니폼을 입은 팬들이 열광적으로 응원하는 것을 볼 수 있다. 눈이 너무 많이 와서 잘 보이지 않아도 그것은 중요하지 않은 것 같다. 미국의 미식축구 팬들은 자신들이 경기 현장에 있어야만 한다고 생각하는 것 같다. 팬들이 경기장에 없으면 선수들이 경기를 잘할 수 없다고 생각하는 것 같다. 그 사람들의 생각이 맞을지도 모른다.

- **정답** > b. American football fans really enjoy watching football games.

Take a break

▶ 영어발음을 향상시키는 방법

apple을 한번 발음해 보세요!

어떤 발음이 나올까요? 많은 한국인들은 [애플]이라고 많이들 발음을 합니다. 하지만 여기에서는 단어 첫 글자인 a가 아주 중요합니다. 이 첫 글자를 강조하면서 발음을 해야 합니다. a를 발음할 때는 입술을 옆으로 살짝 당기면서 cat을 발음할 때처럼 길고 타이트한 소리가 나와야 합니다. 그리고 여기서 한 가지 더 살펴보면, -pple에서는 p 소리를 내면 안 되고 [ㅃ] 발음이 들려야 한다는 것입니다.

Topic 10

LEVEL 2

CRAVING FOR A HOT DOG?

핫도그 먹고 싶으세요?

Step ❶

Understanding

음원을 들으면서 눈으로 읽어 보고,
문제를 통해서 이해했는지 확인해 보세요.

When you visit America, you will like to try new foods. For example, you may order a frankfurter or a wiener. Surprise! When you get your order, it is only a hot dog. Sometimes people call it a dog for short. Americans come from many different countries, so there are different names for hot dogs. Maybe you ordered a "red hot" because you thought it was a new American food. You will be surprised again to find that it is just a hot dog. But you probably won't be surprised that it is yummy!

 윗글의 내용과 일치하지 않는 것은?

ⓐ Wieners can also be called "hot dogs."
ⓑ Only a frankfurter can be called "a dog" for short.
ⓒ A red hot tastes good.
ⓓ A hot dog and a red hot mean the same thing.

Voca. • yummy 맛있는

Step ❷

Listening

이번에는 억양과 끊어 읽기, 연음과 강조어에 대한
강의를 들어 보세요.

/ 끊어 읽기   ∫ ⌐ 억양   **볼드색 강세를 두어 읽는 부분**   ‿ 연음

When you visit America, / you will like ∫ to try new foods.
For example, / you may order ⌐ a frankfurter or a ∫ wiener.
Surprise! ∫
When you get your order, / it is only‿a hot dog.
Sometimes / people call it a dog ∫ for short.
Americans come from many different countries, / so there are different names for ⌐ hot dogs.
Maybe ∫ you ordered a "red hot" / because you thought it was‿a **new** American food.
You will‿be surprised again / to find ∫ that it is **just** a hot dog.
But / you probably ⌐ won't be surprised / that it‿is yummy!

Step ❸

Read Slowly

스스로 끊어 읽기와 억양을 직접 표시하면서,
천천히 큰 소리로 읽어 보세요.

1회 ☐ 2회 ☐ 3회 ☐ 4회 ☐ 5회 ☐ 6회 ☐ 7회 ☐

When you visit America, you will like to try new foods.

For example, you may order a frankfurter or a wiener.

Surprise! When you get your order, it is only a hot dog.

Sometimes people call it a dog for short.

Americans come from many different countries, so there are different names for hot dogs.

Maybe you ordered a "red hot" because you thought it was a new American food.

You will be surprised again to find that it is just a hot dog.

But you probably won't be surprised that it is yummy!

Step ④

Read Normal Speed with shadowing

자신이 생겼다면 이제 내용을 전달하면서 큰 소리로 따라 읽어 보세요.

| 1회 ☐ | 2회 ☐ | 3회 ☐ | 4회 ☐ | 5회 ☐ | 6회 ☐ | 7회 ☐ |

Step ⑤

Speak / Presentation

이제는 아래 글을 완성하면서 큰 소리로 사람들 앞에서 발표해 보세요.

When you visit America, you will like to _____ _____ _____. For example, you may _____ __ frankfurter or a wiener. Surprise! When _____ _____ _____ _____, it is only a hot dog. Sometimes people call it __ _____ _____ _____. Americans _____ _____ _____ different countries, so there are different names for hot dogs. Maybe you ordered a "red hot" because _____ _____ __ _____ __ new American food. You will be surprised _____ __ _____ _____ it is just a hot dog. _____ _____ _____ won't be surprised that it is yummy!

○ Script

미국에 가면 여러분은 새로운 음식을 맛보려고 할 것이다. 예를 들면, 프랭크퍼터나 위너를 주문할 것이다. 그러나 놀라지 마시라! 주문한 음식이 온 것을 보면 그것은 핫도그에 불과하니까. 간단하게 줄여서 "도그"라고 부르는 경우도 있다. 미국인은 여러 다른 나라에서 온 사람들이 많기 때문에 핫도그도 여러 가지로 다르게 부르는 것이다. "레드 핫"이란 음식이 새로운 미국 음식인 줄 알고 주문하는 경우도 있었을 것이다. 그러나 이 경우에도 "핫도그"에 지나지 않는다는 것을 알고 또 놀랄 것이다. 그러나 맛이 있다는 것에는 놀라지 않을 것이다.

● 정답 > b. Only a frankfurter can be called a dog for short.

Take a break

▶ 영어발음을 향상시키는 방법

women이란 단어를 한번 발음해 보세요!

이 단어에서도 중요한 부분은 끝부분입니다. -men은 [맨]이 아니고 [m-in]이라고 i를 짧고 타이트하게 당기면서 발음을 해야 됩니다. 단어의 첫 부분인 wo-도 [w-i]라고 발음해야 합니다. 여기서 i 소리는 짧게 해야 합니다. often을 발음하는 것도 유사한 방법입니다. 여기서는 [오]로 시작하지 말고, [어-fin]이라고 발음을 해야 합니다.

Topic 11

LEVEL 2

STUDENTS WANT TO SHOW THEIR OWN STYLES

학생들은 자기들만의 스타일을 보여 주기를 원한다

Step ❶

Understanding

음원을 들으면서 눈으로 읽어 보고,
문제를 통해서 이해했는지 확인해 보세요.

Many middle and high school students hate to wear a school uniform. They frequently complain, "We wish we could wear something really cool." A group of middle school students recently asked for something different. They said they don't mind wearing the same colors, but they want to wear their own style. They all want a hip-hop style. The principal said she would discuss it with parents.

 윗글의 주제로 알맞은 것은?

ⓐ Students want to change the style of their school uniforms.
ⓑ Stylish uniforms are very common.
ⓒ The principal wants to change the uniforms.
ⓓ Many students think that their uniforms are cool.

 ▪ frequently 자주, 종종

168

Step ❷

Listening

이번에는 억양과 끊어 읽기, 연음과 강조어에 대한 강의를 들어 보세요.

| /끊어 읽기   ∫↘억양   **볼드색** 강세를 두어 읽는 부분   ‿연음 |

Many middle and high school students ↘**hate** to wear a school uniform.

They frequently complain, / "We wish we could wear something really cool."

A group of middle school students / recently asked for something ↘different.

They said ∫they don't mind wearing‿the same colors, / but they want to ↘wear their own style.

They **all** want‿a hip-hop style.

The principal said ↘she would discuss it with parents.

Step ❸

Read Slowly

스스로 끊어 읽기와 억양을 직접 표시하면서,
천천히 큰 소리로 읽어 보세요.

1회 □ 2회 □ 3회 □ 4회 □ 5회 □ 6회 □ 7회 □

Many middle and high school students hate to wear a school uniform.

They frequently complain, "We wish we could wear something really cool."

A group of middle school students recently asked for something different.

They said they don't mind wearing the same colors, but they want to wear their own style.

They all want a hip-hop style.

The principal said she would discuss it with parents.

Step ❹

Read Normal Speed with shadowing

자신이 생겼다면 이제 내용을 전달하면서 큰 소리로 따라 읽어 보세요.

| 1회 ☐ | 2회 ☐ | 3회 ☐ | 4회 ☐ | 5회 ☐ | 6회 ☐ | 7회 ☐ |

Step ❺

Speak / Presentation

이제는 아래 글을 완성하면서 큰 소리로 사람들 앞에서 발표해 보세요.

Many middle and high school students hate ___ _____ ___ _____ uniform. They _____ _____, "We wish we could wear something really cool." A group of middle school students _____ _____ ___ _____ different. They said they don't mind wearing the same colors, but they want to wear ____ ____ ____. ____ ____ ____ a hip-hop style. The principal said ____ _____ _____ ___ with parents.

◦ Script

중·고등학교 학생들 중에는 교복을 입는 것을 아주 싫어하는 학생들이 많다. 그래서 자주 "진짜 멋있는 옷을 입었으면 좋겠어."라고 불평한다. 중학교 학생들이 최근에 좀 색다른 것을 요구한 일이 있었다. 이 학생들은 모두 같은 색의 교복을 입는 것은 괜찮지만 자신들의 스타일로 옷을 입고 싶다고 했다. 모두 힙합 스타일의 교복을 입고 싶어 한다. 교장은 부모들과 이 문제를 의논하겠다고 말했다.

● 정답 > a. Students want to change the style of their school uniforms.

Take a break

▶ 영어발음을 향상시키는 방법

perfect를 한번 발음해 보세요!

어떤 사람들은 [per-팩트]라고 발음을 하지만 -fect를 그대로 발음하지 않고, -fikt 라고 발음하는 것이 더 자연스럽습니다. 이처럼 영어 단어를 제대로 발음하지 않는 경우가 많은데, 꾸준히 연습하면 정확한 발음을 하는 것이 훨씬 쉬워질 것입니다.

Topic 12

LEVEL 2

VEGETABLES ARE GOOD FOR CARS TOO!

야채는 자동차한테도 중요하다!

Step ❶

Understanding

음원을 들으면서 눈으로 읽어 보고,
문제를 통해서 이해했는지 확인해 보세요.

Many people worry about some problems related to cars. One is that cars use gas and oil. If we use too much gas or oil, we won't have enough gas or oil in the future. Another problem is that oil fuels pollute the air. These reasons made some people in the United States use a kind of vegetable fuel for their cars. They found a way to use old vegetable cooking oil as a fuel. A new car in Britain runs on fuel made from rotten vegetables. These various new cars may soon solve our problems.

Q! 다음 글을 읽고 아래 빈칸을 채워 글의 요지를 완성하시오.

Cars that use _____ _____ may solve our problems by saving _____ _____ _____, and reducing air pollution.

Voca. • Britain 영국

Step ❷

Listening

이번에는 억양과 끊어 읽기, 연음과 강조어에 대한 강의를 들어 보세요.

/ 끊어 읽기   ∫ ↘ 억양   볼드색 강세를 두어 읽는 부분   ⌣ 연음

Many people ↘worry about some problems related ∫to cars.
One is that / cars use gas and⌣oil.
If we use **too** much gas or oil, / we⌣won't have ∫enough gas or oil ↘in the future.
Another ∫problem is that / oil fuels pollute ↘the⌣air.
These reasons made some people in the United States ↘use a⌣kind of vegetable fuel / for their cars.
They found a⌣way to use old vegetable cooking oil / as a fuel.
A new ∫car in Britain runs⌣on fuel made from rotten ↘ vegetables.
These various new cars / may **soon** solve our problems.

Step ❸

Read Slowly

스스로 끊어 읽기와 억양을 직접 표시하면서,
천천히 큰 소리로 읽어 보세요.

| 1회 □ | 2회 □ | 3회 □ | 4회 □ | 5회 □ | 6회 □ | 7회 □ |

Many people worry about some problems related to cars.

One is that cars use gas and oil.

If we use too much gas or oil, we won't have enough gas or oil in the future.

Another problem is that oil fuels pollute the air.

These reasons made some people in the United States use a kind of vegetable fuel for their cars.

They found a way to use old vegetable cooking oil as a fuel.

A new car in Britain runs on fuel made from rotten vegetables.

These various new cars may soon solve our problems.

Step ④

Read Normal Speed with shadowing

자신이 생겼다면 이제 내용을 전달하면서 큰 소리로 따라 읽어 보세요.

1회 □   2회 □   3회 □   4회 □   5회 □   6회 □   7회 □

Step ⑤

Speak / Presentation

이제는 아래 글을 완성하면서 큰 소리로 사람들 앞에서 발표해 보세요.

Many people worry about some problems _____ ___ ____.
One is _____ _____ _____ gas and oil. If we use too much
gas or oil, ____ _____ _____ _____ gas or oil in the future.
Another problem is that ____ _____ _____ the air. _____
_____ made some people in the United States use a kind
of vegetable fuel for their cars. They _____ ___ ____ ___
use old vegetable cooking oil as a fuel. A new car in Britain
_____ ____ _____ made from rotten vegetables. _____
_____ ___ ____ may soon solve our problems.

○ Script

많은 사람들이 자동차에 관련된 몇몇 문제들을 걱정한다. 그 중의 한 가지는 자동차가 가스와 기름을 사용하는 문제이다. 가스와 기름을 너무 많이 사용하면 미래에는 가스와 기름이 모자라게 된다. 또 다른 걱정거리는 기름 연료가 대기를 오염시키고 있다는 점이다. 이러한 이유들로 일부 미국 사람들은 일종의 식물성 연료를 만들게 되었다. 식물성 식용유를 자동차 연료로 사용하는 방법을 찾아낸 것이다. 영국에서는 썩은 채소에서 나오는 연료로 가는 차가 새로 등장했다. 이런 여러 가지 새로운 자동차들이 조만간 우리 문제를 해결해 줄지도 모른다.

- 정답 > Cars that use **vegetable fuel** may solve our problems by saving **oil and gas**, and reducing air pollution.

Take a break

▶ 영어발음을 향상시키는 방법

리듬감을 가지세요.

영어를 발음하는 것이 어렵다는 생각은 버리고 가벼운 마음으로 영어에 리듬감을 가지고 자연스럽게 발음해 보세요. 영어발음과 영어표현을 하는 데 큰 도움이 될 수 있습니다. 한국어의 어감과 영어 어감은 많이 다릅니다. 한국말을 할 때에는 주로 한 tone으로 말을 하지만, 영어는 자주 올렸다 내렸다 하는 리듬감이 있습니다. 영어발음을 할 때에는 무엇보다도 자신 있게 말을 하고, 리듬도 많이 연습해 보세요. 더욱 발음을 잘하게 될 것입니다.

Topic 13 LEVEL 2

THE OLYMPIC GAMES WILL BE TREASURED FOREVER

올림픽 게임은 영원한 가치를 지닌다

Step ❶

Understanding

음원을 들으면서 눈으로 읽어 보고,
문제를 통해서 이해했는지 확인해 보세요.

The first Olympic Games were a religious festival for the Greek people. They played games to honor the god Zeus. There was only one sports event in the very early Olympic Games. It was the marathon. In ancient races many people ran without clothes. Today's Olympic Games, however, are an international sports competition. In modern Olympics, athletes wear clothes. Athletes from all over the world try to win medals and honor for their country. There are differences between the first Olympic Games and the modern Olympics, but the athletes in the games have always tried to do their best.

 윗글의 요지를 가장 적절하게 추론한 것은?

ⓐ The Olympic Games of ancient Greece were different from the modern Olympics.
ⓑ Today's Olympic Games are better than the Olympic Games of ancient Greece.
ⓒ Athletes always do their best.
ⓓ The first Olympic games were a religious festival for the Greek people.

 • Greek 그리스의 • race 경주 • modern 현대의

Step ❷

Listening

이번에는 억양과 끊어 읽기, 연음과 강조어에 대한 강의를 들어 보세요.

/ 끊어 읽기   ∫↘ 억양   볼드색 강세를 두어 읽는 부분   ⌣ 연음

The first Olympic Games / were a religious festival ↘for‿the Greek people.

They played games / to honor the god Zeus.

There was only **one** sports event in‿the very early Olympic Games. It was the marathon.

In ancient races ∫ many people ran **without** clothes.

Today's Olympic Games, / however, / are an international ∫ sports ↘competition.

In modern Olympics, / athletes wear clothes.

Athletes from all‿over the world / try to win medals ∫ and honor for their country.

There are differences between ↘the first Olympic Games / and the modern Olympics, but the athletes in the games / have **always** tried to‿do their best.

Step ❸

Read Slowly

스스로 끊어 읽기와 억양을 직접 표시하면서,
천천히 큰 소리로 읽어 보세요.

1회 □ 2회 □ 3회 □ 4회 □ 5회 □ 6회 □ 7회 □

The first Olympic Games were a religious festival for the Greek people.
They played games to honor the god Zeus.
There was only one sports event in the very early Olympic Games.
It was the marathon.
In ancient races many people ran without clothes.
Today's Olympic Games, however, are an international sports competition.
In modern Olympics, athletes wear clothes.
Athletes from all over the world try to win medals and honor for their country.
There are differences between the first Olympic Games and the modern Olympics, but the athletes in the games have always tried to do their best.

Step ❹

Read Normal Speed with shadowing

자신이 생겼다면 이제 내용을 전달하면서 큰 소리로 따라 읽어 보세요.

| 1회 □ | 2회 □ | 3회 □ | 4회 □ | 5회 □ | 6회 □ | 7회 □ |

Step ❺

Speak / Presentation

이제는 아래 글을 완성하면서 큰 소리로 사람들 앞에서 발표해 보세요.

The first Olympic Games were a religious _____ ___ ___ Greek people. They played _____ ___ ___ ___ god Zeus. There ____ _____ ___ sports event in the very early Olympic Games. It was ____ _____. In ancient races _____ _____ _____ without clothes. Today's Olympic Games, however, ___ ___ _____ sports competition. In modern Olympics, _____ ____ clothes. Athletes from all over the world ____ ___ ___ _____ and honor for their country. There ____ _____ between the first Olympic Games and the modern Olympics, but the athletes in the games have _____ ____ ___ ___ their best.

○ Script

최초의 올림픽 경기는 그리스인들의 종교적인 축제였다. 그들은 제우스 신을 찬양하기 위해 게임을 했다. 최초 올림픽 게임에는 한 가지 종목만 있었다. 그것은 바로 마라톤이었다. 고대 경기에서는 많은 사람들이 옷을 입지 않고 달렸다. 그러나 오늘날의 올림픽 게임은 국제적인 스포츠 시합이다. 현대 올림픽에서는 선수들이 옷을 입는다. 각국의 운동선수들은 메달을 따고 본인들의 나라를 명예롭게 하기 위해 노력한다. 최초의 올림픽과 오늘날의 올림픽에는 차이점이 있지만 선수들은 언제나 최선을 다하려고 노력해 왔다.

● 정답 〉 a. The Olympic Games of ancient Greece were different from the modern Olympics.

Take a break

▶ 영어발음을 향상시키는 방법

r 발음하기

한 가지 주의할 점은 어떤 사람들은 r 발음을 너무 굴리려고 하는 경우가 있다는 것입니다. 이렇게 하시면 안 됩니다. 네이티브들에게는 오히려 더 부자연스럽게 들립니다. r 발음을 정확하게 하되 지나치게 오버하지 않도록 조심하세요. 그리고 입술과 혀에 힘을 너무 주지 말고, 가볍고 자연스러운 소리가 나올 수 있도록 해 보세요. 물론 많은 연습이 필요합니다.

Topic 14

LEVEL 2

FLY UP IN A HOT AIR BALLOON

열기구를 타고 하늘로 날아오르자

Step ❶

Understanding

음원을 들으면서 눈으로 읽어 보고,
문제를 통해서 이해했는지 확인해 보세요.

Have you ever had a ride in a hot air balloon? Do you know what a hot air balloon is like? From the ground a hot air balloon looks very small. You know, of course, that is really big. The top part is huge because it needs enough place for hot air to make the balloon go up. Under the big balloon, there's a big burner that makes the air hot. The last part of the balloon is the big basket. People can ride in this big basket made of wicker. Hot air balloons are fun to watch. Some people think they are fun to ride in, too.

 윗글의 주제로 알맞은 것은?

ⓐ Why people like to ride in a hot air balloon
ⓑ What hot air balloons are like
ⓒ Where hot air balloons are found
ⓓ How hot air balloons were made

 • hot air balloon 열기구 • burner 연소기

Step ❷

Listening

이번에는 억양과 끊어 읽기, 연음과 강조어에 대한 강의를 들어 보세요.

/ 끊어 읽기   ↗ ↘ 억양   **볼드색 강세를 두어 읽는 부분**   ‿ 연음

Have you ↗ ever had a ride in‿a hot air balloon? ↗

Do you know ↘ what a hot air balloon is like? ↗

From the ground / a hot air balloon looks very‿small.

You know, / of **course**, / that is **really** big.

The top part ↘ is huge / because it needs enough place for hot air / to make the‿balloon go up.

Under the big balloon, / there's a big burner ↘ that makes the air hot.

The last ↗ part of‿the balloon / is the big basket.

People ↗ can ride in this big basket / made of wicker.

Hot air balloons / are fun to watch.

Some people think / they ↗ are fun to ride in, / too.

Step ❸

Read Slowly

스스로 끊어 읽기와 억양을 직접 표시하면서,
천천히 큰 소리로 읽어 보세요.

1회 □   2회 □   3회 □   4회 □   5회 □   6회 □   7회 □

Have you ever had a ride in a hot air balloon?

Do you know what a hot air balloon is like?

From the ground a hot air balloon looks very small.

You know, of course, that is really big.

The top part is huge because it needs enough place for hot air to make the balloon go up.

Under the big balloon, there's a big burner that makes the air hot.

The last part of the balloon is the big basket.

People can ride in this big basket made of wicker.

Hot air balloons are fun to watch.

Some people think they are fun to ride in, too.

Step ❹

Read Normal Speed with shadowing

자신이 생겼다면 이제 내용을 전달하면서 큰 소리로 따라 읽어 보세요.

1회 ☐ 2회 ☐ 3회 ☐ 4회 ☐ 5회 ☐ 6회 ☐ 7회 ☐

Step ❺

Speak / Presentation

이제는 아래 글을 완성하면서 큰 소리로 사람들 앞에서 발표해 보세요.

Have you ever had ___ ____ ___ __ hot air balloon? Do you know what a hot air _____ __ ____? _____ ____ _____ a hot air balloon looks very small. You know, of course, that ____ _____ big. The top part is ____ _____ ___ needs enough place for hot air to make the balloon go up. Under the big balloon, there's a big burner that _____ ____ ___ ____. The _____ _____ ___ ____ balloon is the big basket. _____ ____ _____ in this big basket made of wicker. Hot air balloons ____ ____ _____ watch. _____ _____ _____ they are fun to ride in, too.

○ Script

열기구를 타 본 적이 있는가? 열기구가 어떻게 생겼는지 알고 있는가? 지상에서 보면 열기구는 아주 작게 보인다. 물론 실제로는 엄청나게 크다는 것을 알 수 있다. 기구의 윗부분은 엄청나게 큰데 기구가 공중에 뜨도록 하는 데 필요한 뜨거운 공기가 들어갈 충분한 공간이 필요하기 때문이다. 큰 풍선 아래에는 공기를 덥히는 연소기가 달려 있다. 기구의 마지막 부분은 큰 바구니다. 사람들은 가지로 엮은 이 커다란 바구니에 타게 된다. 열기구를 보는 것은 재미있다. 그리고 타는 것도 재미있다고 생각하는 사람들도 있다.

- 정답 > b. What hot air balloons are like

Take a break

▶ 영어발음을 향상시키는 방법

단어 발음에 자신이 없다면?

많은 사람들이 영어 단어에 자신이 없을 때에 자신의 목소리를 낮추어 발음해서 제대로 안 들리는 경우가 많습니다. 그럴 때일수록 더 자신감을 가지고 크게 말해 보세요. 그렇게 하면 듣는 사람의 입장에서는 발음이 좀 틀리더라도 감을 잡아서 이해를 할 때가 많습니다. 반대로 목소리를 더 줄여서 낮은 소리로 단어를 말하면, 발음도 틀렸지만 소리조차 들리지 않아서 의사 전달이 전혀 되지 않을 수 있습니다. 자신 있게 당당하게 영어로 말하고, 발음이 틀리면 고쳐 나가는 것이 다음에 더 잘할 수 있는 방법입니다.

Topic 15

LEVEL 2

FLYING MAMMALS

날아다니는 포유동물

Step ❶

Understanding

음원을 들으면서 눈으로 읽어 보고,
문제를 통해서 이해했는지 확인해 보세요.

Bats can fly, but they are different from birds. Bats are mammals. This means bats are born from their mother's body. They are born alive, just like kittens or human babies. Birds lay eggs and then later baby birds come out of the eggs. Bats get milk from their mom. Bird moms drop worms into their babies' mouths. Bats have fur. Birds have feathers, not fur or hair. In fact, bats and birds are very different. Bats are more like people than like birds. Bats have arms, hands, and feet. However, bats are the only mammals that fly.

 윗글의 주제로 알맞은 것은?

ⓐ Differences between bats and mammals
ⓑ Differences between birds and bats
ⓒ Differences between bird moms and worms
ⓓ Differences between birds and mammals

- kitten 새끼 고양이
- mammal 포유동물

Step ❷

Listening

이번에는 억양과 끊어 읽기, 연음과 강조어에 대한
강의를 들어 보세요.

> / 끊어 읽기   ∫↘ 억양   **볼드색** 강세를 두어 읽는 부분   ‿ 연음

Bats can fly, / but they ∫ are different from birds.
Bats are mammals.
This means / bats are born from their mother's ∫ body.
They are born alive, / **just** like kittens / or human ↘babies.
Birds lay eggs / and then later / baby birds come out of‿the eggs.
Bats get milk / from their mom.
Bird moms drop ↘worms into their babies' mouths.
Bats have fur.
Birds have ↘feathers, / not fur or hair.
In fact, / bats and birds / are **very** different.
Bats ∫ are more like people ↘than like birds.
Bats have arms, / hands, / and feet.
However, / bats are‿the **only** mammals / that fly.

Step ❸

Read Slowly

스스로 끊어 읽기와 억양을 직접 표시하면서,
천천히 큰 소리로 읽어 보세요.

1회 ☐ 2회 ☐ 3회 ☐ 4회 ☐ 5회 ☐ 6회 ☐ 7회 ☐

Bats can fly, but they are different from birds.

Bats are mammals.

This means bats are born from their mother's body.

They are born alive, just like kittens or human babies.

Birds lay eggs and then later baby birds come out of the eggs.

Bats get milk from their mom.

Bird moms drop worms into their babies' mouths.

Bats have fur.

Birds have feathers, not fur or hair.

In fact, bats and birds are very different.

Bats are more like people than like birds.

Bats have arms, hands, and feet.

However, bats are the only mammals that fly.

Step ④

Read Normal Speed with shadowing
자신이 생겼다면 이제 내용을 전달하면서 큰 소리로 따라 읽어 보세요.

1회 □   2회 □   3회 □   4회 □   5회 □   6회 □   7회 □

Step ⑤

Speak / Presentation
이제는 아래 글을 완성하면서 큰 소리로 사람들 앞에서 발표해 보세요.

Bats can fly, but they are _____ _____ _____. Bats _____ _____. This means _____ _____ _____ _____ their mother's body. They are born alive, _____ _____ _____ _____ human babies. Birds lay eggs and then later baby birds _____ _____ _____ _____ eggs. _____ _____ _____ from their mom. Bird moms _____ _____ _____ _____ babies' mouths. Bats have fur. _____ _____ _____, not fur or hair. In fact, _____ _____ _____ are very different. Bats are more like people _____ _____ _____. Bats _____ _____, _____, and feet. However, bats are the _____ _____ _____ _____.

○ Script

박쥐는 날 수 있지만 새와는 다르다. 박쥐는 포유동물이다. 이 말은 박쥐는 어미의 몸에서 태어난다는 뜻이다. 박쥐는 새끼 고양이나 인간의 아기처럼 산 채로 태어난다. 새는 알을 낳고, 나중에 그 알에서 새가 나온다. 박쥐는 어미의 젖을 먹는다. 어미 새는 새끼의 입 속에다 벌레를 떨어뜨려 준다. 박쥐는 털이 있다. 새는 깃털이 있지, 털이나 머리카락이 없다. 사실 박쥐와 새는 아주 다르다. 박쥐는 새보다 인간과 많이 닮았다. 박쥐에게는 팔, 손, 발이 있다. 그러나, 박쥐만이 유일하게 날 수 있는 포유동물이다.

● 정답 > b. Differences between birds and bats

Take a break

▶ 영어발음을 향상시키는 방법

영어발음을 연습하는 비법

영어를 할 때에는 입과 입술을 많이 움직여야 하므로 가끔 거울 앞에서 입을 풀고 연습해 보세요. 그리고 alphabet를 A부터 Z까지 몇 번 말해 보세요! 때로는 한 문장을 영어로 수차례 반복해서 소리 내며 발음을 해 보는 것도 도움이 됩니다. 그리고 이런 연습 내용을 녹음해서 들어 보고 어색하게 들리는 부분이 있으면 자연스러워질 때까지 반복해서 연습해 보세요. 이처럼 즐기는 마음으로 발음 연습을 계속한다면 여러분도 완벽한 영어발음을 하실 수 있습니다. 시간이 좀 걸리더라도 한번 도전해 보세요.

READ ALOUD

LEVEL 3

LEVEL 3

Topic no.	Title
01	Do You Know Who Philip Ahn Is?
02	Deja Vu
03	Some Facts About Penguins
04	The Invention Of The E-mail
05	Fashion Trends
06	Fall In Love
07	Fish That Break Wind
08	The Colorful Rainbow
09	The Blue Sky
10	The Importance Of Water
11	Natural Foods Prevent Us From Getting Sick
12	Alfred Nobel
13	The Bridal Shower
14	Get Away From The Indoor Air Pollutants
15	What Is A Piggy Bank?

Topic 01   LEVEL 3

DO YOU KNOW WHO PHILIP AHN IS?

필립 안이 누구인지 아나요?

Step ❶

Understanding

음원을 들으면서 눈으로 읽어 보고,
문제를 통해서 이해했는지 확인해 보세요.

Many Koreans do not know Philip Ahn. He was the son of Dosan Ahn Chang Ho. Philip was the first American citizen born of Korean parents in the United States. He was the first Korean to become well-known in American movies. Philip played hundreds of film roles with many famous American stars. He had a long film career. Philip also had a part on a popular TV show. He played Master Kan, leader of the Shaolin Temple in the ABC TV series, Kung Fu. Philip Ahn died in 1978. In 1984, a star was put on the Hollywood Walk of Fame to honor Mr. Ahn.

 윗글의 주제로 알맞은 것은?
ⓐ The life of Philip Ahn
ⓑ Philip Ahn's film career
ⓒ Philip Ahn's mother
ⓓ Philip Ahn's father

Voca. • career 경력

Step ❷

Listening

이번에는 억양과 끊어 읽기, 연음과 강조어에 대한 강의를 들어 보세요.

/ 끊어 읽기   ∫↘ 억양   **볼드색** 강세를 두어 읽는 부분   ‿ 연음

Many Koreans do not know ↘ Philip Ahn.

He was the son of / Dosan Ahn Chang Ho.

Philip was the **first** American citizen / born of Korean parents in‿the United States.

He ∫ was the first Korean to become / well-known in American ↘ movies.

Philip played **hundreds** of film roles / with many famous American stars.

He had‿a **long** film career.

Philip also / had‿a part on‿a popular TV show.

He played Master Kan, / leader of‿the Shaolin Temple / in‿the ABC TV series, / Kung Fu.

Philip Ahn died‿in 1978.

In 1984, / a star was put on‿the Hollywood Walk of Fame / to honor Mr. Ahn.

Step ❸

Read Slowly

스스로 끊어 읽기와 억양을 직접 표시하면서,
천천히 큰 소리로 읽어 보세요.

1회 □　2회 □　3회 □　4회 □　5회 □　6회 □　7회 □

Many Koreans do not know Philip Ahn.

He was the son of Dosan Ahn Chang Ho.

Philip was the first American citizen born of Korean parents in the United States.

He was the first Korean to become well-known in American movies.

Philip played hundreds of film roles with many famous American stars.

He had a long film career.

Philip also had a part on a popular TV show.

He played Master Kan, leader of the Shaolin Temple in the ABC TV series, Kung Fu.

Philip Ahn died in 1978.

In 1984, a star was put on the Hollywood Walk of Fame to honor Mr. Ahn.

Step ④

Read Normal Speed with shadowing
자신이 생겼다면 이제 내용을 전달하면서 큰 소리로 따라 읽어 보세요.

1회 □ 2회 □ 3회 □ 4회 □ 5회 □ 6회 □ 7회 □

Step ⑤

Speak / Presentation
이제는 아래 글을 완성하면서 큰 소리로 사람들 앞에서 발표해 보세요.

Many Koreans ___ ___ ___ Philip Ahn. He ___ ___ ___ ___ Dosan Ahn Chang Ho. Philip was the first American _____ ___ ___ Korean parents in the United States. He was the first Korean ___ ___ _____ in American movies. Philip played hundreds of film roles _____ _____ _____ American stars. ____ ___ __ ____ film career. Philip also had a _____ ___ ___ _____ TV show. He played Master Kan, _____ ___ ___ Shaolin Temple in the ABC TV series, Kung Fu. Philip Ahn died in 1978. In 1984, a star ____ ____ ___ ___ Hollywood Walk of Fame to honor Mr. Ahn.

⊙ Script

필립 안에 대해서 아는 한국인들은 많지 않다. 이 사람은 도산 안창호의 아들이다. 필립은 미국에서 한국인 부모에게 태어난 최초의 미국 시민이다. 그는 미국 영화에 출연해 잘 알려진 최초의 한국인이었다. 필립은 여러 유명한 미국 스타들과 함께 수백 편의 영화에 출연했다. 이 사람은 오랫동안 영화계에 종사했다. 필립은 텔레비전 프로에서 역할을 맡기도 했다. ABC TV의 "쿵후" 시리즈에서 소림사의 지도자인 칸 사부의 역할을 했다. 필립은 1978년에 죽었다. 1984년에는 필립 안을 기리기 위해서 할리우드의 명예의 길에 별이 새겨졌다.

- 정답 > a. The life of Philip Ahn

Take a break

▶ 영어발음을 향상시키는 방법

TONGUE TWISTER : 주의점은 fl-의 발음

A flea and a fly in a flue

Said the fly "Oh what should we do?"

Said the flea "Let us fly."

Said the fly "Let us flee."

So they flew through a flaw in the flue.

Topic 02

LEVEL 3

DEJA VU

데자뷰

Step ❶

Understanding

음원을 들으면서 눈으로 읽어 보고,
문제를 통해서 이해했는지 확인해 보세요.

The term deja vu comes from the French and means already seen. Although as much as 70 percent of society claims to have experienced some form of deja vu in their lives, we still know very little about it. People who have experienced deja vu say that it is like an overwhelming sense of familiarity with something that shouldn't be familiar at all. There are many questions about how and why deja vu happens. Several psychoanalysts think that it is simple fantasy or wish fulfillment, while some psychiatrists believe it is the brain mistaking the present for the past.

 윗글의 내용으로 볼 때, 정신과 의사들이 생각하는 데자뷰 현상의 원인은?

ⓐ It occurs to people who are under great pressure.
ⓑ It is a temporary disease.
ⓒ It is the brain mistaking the present for the past.
ⓓ It is simple fantasy or wish fulfillment.

 • overwhelming 압도적인   • wish fulfillment 소원 성취

Step ❷

Listening

이번에는 억양과 끊어 읽기, 연음과 강조어에 대한 강의를 들어 보세요.

/ 끊어 읽기   ∫⌐ 억양   볼드색 강세를 두어 읽는 부분   ‿ 연음

The term deja vu / comes from the French / and means / already seen.

Although / as much as 70 percent of society / claims to‿have experienced / some form of deja vu in their lives, / we still know ⌐very little about it.

People ∫who have experienced deja vu / say that it is like‿an overwhelming sense of familiarity / with something / that shouldn't be familiar at‿all.

There are **many** questions about how and why ⌐deja vu happens.
Several psychoanalysts think that / it is simple fantasy or wish ⌐ fulfillment, / while **some** psychiatrists ∫believe / it is the brain mistaking the present for‿the past.

Step ❸

Read Slowly

스스로 끊어 읽기와 억양을 직접 표시하면서,
천천히 큰 소리로 읽어 보세요.

1회 □ 2회 □ 3회 □ 4회 □ 5회 □ 6회 □ 7회 □

The term deja vu comes from the French and means already seen.
Although as much as 70 percent of society claims to have experienced some form of deja vu in their lives, we still know very little about it.
People who have experienced deja vu say that it is like an overwhelming sense of familiarity with something that shouldn't be familiar at all.
There are many questions about how and why deja vu happens.
Several psychoanalysts think that it is simple fantasy or wish fulfillment, while some psychiatrists believe it is the brain mistaking the present for the past.

Step ❹

Read Normal Speed with shadowing

자신이 생겼다면 이제 내용을 전달하면서 큰 소리로 따라 읽어 보세요.

1회 ☐ 2회 ☐ 3회 ☐ 4회 ☐ 5회 ☐ 6회 ☐ 7회 ☐

Step ❺

Speak / Presentation

이제는 아래 글을 완성하면서 큰 소리로 사람들 앞에서 발표해 보세요.

The term deja vu comes from the French and _____ _____ _____. Although as much as 70 percent _____ _____ _____ ___ have experienced some form of deja vu in their lives, we still know very little about it. _____ _____ _____ experienced deja vu say that it is like an overwhelming sense of familiarity with something that shouldn't be familiar at all. There are _____ _____ _____ _____ and why deja vu happens. Several psychoanalysts think that it is _____ _____ ___ wish fulfillment, while some psychiatrists believe it is the brain mistaking the present for the past.

● Script

데자뷰라는 용어는 프랑스 어에서 유래된 것으로, "이미 봤다"는 의미이다. 어떤 사회든 70%나 되는 사람들이 살면서 어떤 식으로든 데자뷰를 경험해 봤다고 주장하지만, 아직 데자뷰에 대해 우리가 아는 것은 거의 없다. 데자뷰를 경험한 사람들은 결코 친숙한 것일 리가 없는 것이 너무나 친숙하게 느껴지는 감정이라고 말한다. 이 현상이 어떻게, 왜 일어나는지에 대해서는 의문점이 많다. 정신분석가들 중에는 이 현상은 단순한 환상이나 소망 성취라고 보는 사람들이 있는 반면, 정신과 의사들 중에는 이것이 현재를 과거로 착각하는 두뇌의 착오라고 생각하는 사람들이 있다.

● 정답 > c. It is the brain mistaking the present for the past.

Take a break

▶ 영어발음을 향상시키는 방법

TONGUE TWISTER : 주의점은 p와 r의 발음

Peter Piper picked a peck of pickled peppers.

A peck of pickled peppers Peter Piper picked.

If Peter Piper picked a peck of pickled peppers,

Where's the peck of pickled peppers Peter Piper picked?

Topic 03 LEVEL 3

SOME FACTS ABOUT PENGUINS

펭귄에 대한 사실들

Step ❶

Understanding

음원을 들으면서 눈으로 읽어 보고,
문제를 통해서 이해했는지 확인해 보세요.

Penguins live in many different places and raise their own children. Most penguins live in Antarctica, but many others live in South Africa, the Galapagos Islands (off Ecuador), and even the islands of Australia. Baby penguins hatch from eggs. The parents make a nest out of very small rocks and mud. The baby gets its food from the mother or father; the parents chew up food and let the baby eat the food that is inside their mouths. Penguins need to eat at least twice a day and they like to eat fish, shrimp, and krill.

 윗글의 내용과 일치하는 것은?
ⓐ Penguins don't raise their own children.
ⓑ Penguins only eat fresh fish and shrimp.
ⓒ Penguins need to eat at least three times a day.
ⓓ Penguins make a nest with very small rocks and mud.

 • hatch 부화하다   • chew up 음식을 씹다

Step ❷

Listening

이번에는 억양과 끊어 읽기, 연음과 강조어에 대한 강의를 들어 보세요.

/ 끊어 읽기   ∫↘ 억양   **볼드색** 강세를 두어 읽는 부분   ‿ 연음

Penguins live in many ∫ different places and raise their‿own children.
Most penguins live‿in Antarctica, / but **many** others live in ↘
South Africa, / the Galapagos Islands (off Ecuador), / and **even** the islands of ↘ Australia.
Baby penguins hatch‿from eggs.
The parents make a nest out of / very small rocks ↘ and mud.
The baby ∫ gets its food from the mother or‿father; / the parents ∫ chew up food / and let the baby eat the food that‿is inside **their** mouths.
Penguins need to eat **at least** twice a day / and they like‿to eat fish, / shrimp, / and krill.

Step ❸

Read Slowly

스스로 끊어 읽기와 억양을 직접 표시하면서,
천천히 큰 소리로 읽어 보세요.

| 1회 ☐ 2회 ☐ 3회 ☐ 4회 ☐ 5회 ☐ 6회 ☐ 7회 ☐ |

Penguins live in many different places and raise their own children.
Most penguins live in Antarctica, but many others live in South Africa, the Galapagos Islands (off Ecuador), and even the islands of Australia.
Baby penguins hatch from eggs.
The parents make a nest out of very small rocks and mud.
The baby gets its food from the mother or father; the parents chew up food and let the baby eat the food that is inside their mouths.
Penguins need to eat at least twice a day and they like to eat fish, shrimp, and krill.

Step ❹

Read Normal Speed with shadowing

자신이 생겼다면 이제 내용을 전달하면서 큰 소리로 따라 읽어 보세요.

1회 ☐ 2회 ☐ 3회 ☐ 4회 ☐ 5회 ☐ 6회 ☐ 7회 ☐

Step ❺

Speak / Presentation

이제는 아래 글을 완성하면서 큰 소리로 사람들 앞에서 발표해 보세요.

Penguins live in many different places and _____ _____ _____ children. Most _____ ____ in Antarctica, but many others live in South Africa, the Galapagos Islands (off Ecuador), and even the islands of Australia. ____ _____ _____ from eggs. The parents make a nest out of very _____ _____ _____ _____. The baby _____ ___ _____ _____ the mother or father; the parents chew up food and let the baby eat the food that is inside their mouths. Penguins need to _____ ___ _____ twice a day and they like ___ _____ _____, shrimp, and krill.

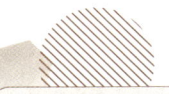

○ Script

펭귄은 여러 다른 지역에서 살며, 새끼를 기르는 동물이다. 대부분 남극 대륙에서 살지만, 남아프리카 공화국, 에콰도르 앞바다에 있는 갈라파고스 제도, 심지어는 오스트레일리아의 섬에도 많이 살고 있다. 펭귄 새끼는 알에서 부화한다. 펭귄 부모는 아주 작은 돌과 진흙으로 둥지를 만든다. 새끼는 어머니나 아버지에게 음식을 받아먹는데, 부모가 음식을 씹어 입안에 넣고 있으면 새끼가 부모의 입에서 그것을 받아먹는다. 펭귄은 하루에 적어도 두 번 먹어야 하는데, 물고기, 새우, 크릴을 좋아한다.

● 정답 〉 d. Penguins make a nest with very small rocks and mud.

Take a break

▶ 영어발음을 향상시키는 방법

TONGUE TWISTER : 주의점은 -oard의 발음

How many boards

Could the Mongols hoard

If the Mongol hordes got bored?

Topic 04

LEVEL 3

THE INVENTION OF THE E-MAIL

이메일의 출현

Step ❶

Understanding

음원을 들으면서 눈으로 읽어 보고,
문제를 통해서 이해했는지 확인해 보세요.

The first electronic message, what is known as e-mail, was sent in 1972 by Ray Tomlinson. Tomlinson used the @ symbol to indicate the location or institution of the person receiving the e-mail. Tomlinson understood that he needed to use a symbol that would not appear in anyone's name, so that there would be no confusion. The choice Tomlinson settled on was the @ sign. That is because it wouldn't be in anyone's name and also because it represented the word "at", as if a particular user is sitting at(@) a specific computer.

Q! 윗글의 주제로 알맞은 것은?
ⓐ The first e-mail
ⓑ The @ sign
ⓒ Ray Tomlinson
ⓓ A particular user

 Voca. • institution 기관   • represent 나타내다

Step ❷

Listening

이번에는 억양과 끊어 읽기, 연음과 강조어에 대한 강의를 들어 보세요.

/ 끊어 읽기 ∫↘ 억양   **볼드색 강세를 두어 읽는 부분**   ‿ 연음

The first electronic message, / what is ↘known as e-mail, / was sent ∫ in 1972 by Ray Tomlinson.

Tomlinson used the @ symbol / to indicate the location ↘or institution of‿the person receiving the e-mail.

Tomlinson understood ∫ that he needed to use‿a symbol that would **not** appear in anyone's name, / so‿that there would be no ↘confusion.

The choice Tomlinson settled ∫on / was the @ sign.

That is because / it wouldn't be‿in **anyone's** name / and **also** because it represented / the word "at", / as if a ↘particular user is sitting‿at(@) a specific computer.

Step ❸

Read Slowly

스스로 끊어 읽기와 억양을 직접 표시하면서,
천천히 큰 소리로 읽어 보세요.

1회 ☐ 2회 ☐ 3회 ☐ 4회 ☐ 5회 ☐ 6회 ☐ 7회 ☐

The first electronic message, what is known as e-mail, was sent in 1972 by Ray Tomlinson.

Tomlinson used the @ symbol to indicate the location or institution of the person receiving the e-mail.

Tomlinson understood that he needed to use a symbol that would not appear in anyone's name, so that there would be no confusion.

The choice Tomlinson settled on was the @ sign.

That is because it wouldn't be in anyone's name and also because it represented the word "at", as if a particular user is sitting at(@) a specific computer.

Step ❹

Read Normal Speed with shadowing

자신이 생겼다면 이제 내용을 전달하면서 큰 소리로 따라 읽어 보세요.

1회 ☐ 2회 ☐ 3회 ☐ 4회 ☐ 5회 ☐ 6회 ☐ 7회 ☐

Step ❺

Speak / Presentation

이제는 아래 글을 완성하면서 큰 소리로 사람들 앞에서 발표해 보세요.

The _____ _____ _____, what is known as e-mail, was sent in 1972 by Ray Tomlinson. Tomlinson used the @ symbol to indicate the location or institution of the person receiving the e-mail. Tomlinson understood that he needed to _____ ___ _____ _____ would not appear in anyone's name, so that there would be no confusion. The choice Tomlinson _____ ___ _____ the @ sign. That is because it wouldn't be in anyone's name and also because ___ _____ ____ word "at", as if a particular user is sitting at(@) a specific computer.

○ Script

이메일로 알려져 있는 최초의 전자 메시지는 1972년 레이 톰린슨이란 사람이 처음으로 보냈다. 톰린슨은 이메일 수신자의 위치나 소속 기관을 나타내기 위해 @ 기호를 사용했다. 톰린슨은 사람의 이름에는 쓰이지 않아 그 어떤 혼동도 일으키지 않는 특정 기호를 사용해야 함을 알았다. 톰린슨의 선택은 @ 기호였다. 그 이유는 그 기호가 사람의 이름에 사용되지 않으며, 특정 사용자가 특정한 컴퓨터 앞에 앉아 있음을 나타내는 단어 "~에"(at)를 나타내기 때문이다.

● 정답 > b. The @ sign

Take a break

▶ 영어발음을 향상시키는 방법

TONGUE TWISTER : 주의점은 -eece 와 -eeze의 발음 차이

Denise sees the fleece.

Denise sees the fleas.

At least Denise could sneeze

and feed and freeze the fleas.

Topic 05

LEVEL 3

FASHION TRENDS

패션 트렌드

Step ❶

Understanding

음원을 들으면서 눈으로 읽어 보고,
문제를 통해서 이해했는지 확인해 보세요.

It's so hard to keep up with all the current fashion trends. I go to a public school in downtown New York City, where there are a lot of people from around the world, so there are many different fashion styles. These days, for example, it's very popular for the girls to wear really short skirts and tight tops. For boys, a lot of them are wearing loose jeans or pants, baseball hats and oversize shirts. What's popular with both sexes is retro clothing. Boys and girls are wearing a lot of older clothing nowadays that was cool in the 60s, 70s, and 80s.

Q! 윗글을 읽고 최근 유행하는 패션 스타일을 아래 보기에서 골라 써 넣으시오.

| short skirts | baseball hats | oversize shirts |
| tight tops | loose jeans or pants | |

Boy's Style : _____

Girl's Style : _____

Voca. • downtown 번화가   • cool 인기 있는

Step ❷

Listening

이번에는 억양과 끊어 읽기, 연음과 강조어에 대한 강의를 들어 보세요.

/ 끊어 읽기   ∫↘ 억양   볼드색 강세를 두어 읽는 부분   ‿ 연음

It's **so** hard to keep up with all‿the current ↘ fashion trends.
I go to‿a public school in downtown / New York City, /
where there are a lot‿of people from around the world, /
so ∫ there are **many** different fashion styles.
These days, / for example, / it's **very** popular for the girls ∫ to
wear **really** short skirts / and tight tops.
For boys, / a lot of‿them are wearing loose jeans / or pants, /
baseball hats / **and** oversize shirts.
What's popular with‿both sexes is / retro clothing.
Boys and girls are wearing / a lot‿of older clothing nowadays /
that was cool in‿the 60s, / 70s, / and 80s.

Step ❸

Read Slowly

스스로 끊어 읽기와 억양을 직접 표시하면서,
천천히 큰 소리로 읽어 보세요.

1회 □   2회 □   3회 □   4회 □   5회 □   6회 □   7회 □

It's so hard to keep up with all the current fashion trends.

I go to a public school in downtown New York City, where there are a lot of people from around the world, so there are many different fashion styles.

These days, for example, it's very popular for the girls to wear really short skirts and tight tops.

For boys, a lot of them are wearing loose jeans or pants, baseball hats and oversize shirts.

What's popular with both sexes is retro clothing.

Boys and girls are wearing a lot of older clothing nowadays that was cool in the 60s, 70s, and 80s.

Step ④

Read Normal Speed with shadowing
자신이 생겼다면 이제 내용을 전달하면서 큰 소리로 따라 읽어 보세요.

1회 □ 2회 □ 3회 □ 4회 □ 5회 □ 6회 □ 7회 □

Step ⑤

Speak / Presentation
이제는 아래 글을 완성하면서 큰 소리로 사람들 앞에서 발표해 보세요.

It's so hard to _____ ___ _____ all the current fashion trends. I go to a public school in downtown New York City, where there are a lot of _____ _____ _____ the world, so there are many different fashion styles. _____ _____, for example, it's very popular for the girls to wear really short skirts and tight tops. For boys, a lot of them are wearing _____ _____ ___ _____, baseball hats and oversize shirts. What's popular with both sexes ____ _____ _____. Boys and girls are wearing a lot of older clothing nowadays _____ _____ _____ ___ the 60s, 70s, and 80s.

○ Script

최신 패션 경향을 따라가는 것은 정말 어려운 일이다. 나는 뉴욕의 번화가에 있는 공립학교에 다니는데, 뉴욕은 전 세계에서 온 많은 사람들이 모여 있는 곳이라 다양한 패션 스타일이 많다. 예를 들어, 요즘 여자아이들에게 인기 있는 스타일은 아주 짧은 미니스커트와 꽉 끼는 탑이고, 남자아이들은 헐렁한 청바지나 바지, 야구모자와 특대 사이즈의 셔츠를 많이 입는다. 남녀를 불문하고 인기 있는 스타일은 레트로 풍의 옷들이다. 요즘 남자아이들과 여자아이들은 과거 60년대, 70년대, 80년대에 인기 있었던 복고 스타일 옷들을 많이 입고 다닌다.

- **정답 >** Boy's Style : baseball hats, loose jeans or pants, oversize shirts
  Girl's Style : short skirts, tight tops

Take a break

▶ 영어발음을 향상시키는 방법

TONGUE TWISTER : 주의점은 fi-의 발음

There was a fisherman named Fisher

Who fished for some fish in a fissure.

Till a fish with a grin,

Pulled the fisherman in.

Now they're fishing the fissure for Fisher.

Topic 06

LEVEL 3

FALL IN LOVE

사랑에 빠지다

Step ❶

Understanding

음원을 들으면서 눈으로 읽어 보고,
문제를 통해서 이해했는지 확인해 보세요.

Love is good for you. Not just in the romantic way that many people think. Researchers in Paris have recently concluded a study people who claimed to be in love were actually healthier than those who were not. A majority of the people who were in love with their partner showed several physical signs of being healthier in the study. The signs of being healthy ranged from clear skin to a low rate of common illnesses, like colds and the flu. Researchers say part of this probably has to do with the fact that people in love are happy and positive about life.

 윗글의 요지로 알맞은 것은?

ⓐ Lots of people are in love with their partner.
ⓑ To be healthy, you should find true love.
ⓒ You should find out what to do to be healthy.
ⓓ People in love are healthier than those who are not.

Voca. • illness 질병   • positive 긍정적인

Step ❷

Listening

이번에는 억양과 끊어 읽기, 연음과 강조어에 대한 강의를 들어 보세요.

/ 끊어 읽기   ∫↘ 억양   **볼드색** 강세를 두어 읽는 부분   ‿ 연음

Love‿is good for you.
Not ∫just in‿the romantic way / that many people think.
Researchers in Paris / have recently concluded ↘a study / people who claimed to be in love / were **actually** healthier than‿those who were not.
A majority of‿the people who were in love with their partner / showed **several** physical signs of being healthier ∫in‿the study.
The signs of being healthy ↘ranged from clear skin / to‿a low rate of common illnesses, / like colds and‿the flu.
Researchers say / part of this probably has to do ↘with‿the fact **that** people in‿love are / happy and positive about life.

Step ❸

Read Slowly

스스로 끊어 읽기와 억양을 직접 표시하면서,
천천히 큰 소리로 읽어 보세요.

1회 □ 2회 □ 3회 □ 4회 □ 5회 □ 6회 □ 7회 □

Love is good for you.

Not just in the romantic way that many people think.

Researchers in Paris have recently concluded a study people who claimed to be in love were actually healthier than those who were not.

A majority of the people who were in love with their partner showed several physical signs of being healthier in the study.

The signs of being healthy ranged from clear skin to a low rate of common illnesses, like colds and the flu.

Researchers say part of this probably has to do with the fact that people in love are happy and positive about life.

Step ❹

Read Normal Speed with shadowing
자신이 생겼다면 이제 내용을 전달하면서 큰 소리로 따라 읽어 보세요.

1회 ☐ **2회** ☐ **3회** ☐ **4회** ☐ **5회** ☐ **6회** ☐ **7회** ☐

Step ❺

Speak / Presentation
이제는 아래 글을 완성하면서 큰 소리로 사람들 앞에서 발표해 보세요.

Love is _____ _____ _____. Not _____ ___ _____ _____ way that many people think. Researchers in Paris have recently _____ ___ _____ people who claimed to be in love were actually healthier than those who were not. ___ _____ ____ _____ people who were in love with their partner showed several physical signs of being healthier in the study. The signs of being healthy _____ _____ _____ _____ to a low rate of common illnesses, like colds and the flu. _____ _____ part of this probably has to do with the fact that people in love are happy and positive about life.

○ Script

사랑은 좋은 것이다. 많은 사람들이 생각하듯 그저 낭만적이기 때문만은 아니다. 파리의 연구자들은 최근 한 연구를 마쳤는데, 그 연구를 통해 사랑에 빠졌다고 하는 사람들이 그렇지 않은 사람들에 비해 실제로 더 건강하다는 결과를 얻었다. 연구에서 파트너와 사랑에 빠져 있다고 대답한 대다수의 사람들은 건강하다는 것을 보여 주는 여러 신체적인 표시를 가지고 있는 것으로 나타났다. 건강하다는 표시는 깨끗한 피부에서 감기나 독감 같은 일반적인 질병에 걸릴 확률이 낮은 것까지에 걸쳐 있었다. 이것은 아마도 사랑에 빠진 사람들은 행복하고 인생에 대해 긍정적이라는 사실과 일부 연관을 갖고 있을 것이라고 연구자들은 말한다.

● 정답 > d. People in love are healthier than those who are not.

Take a break

▶ 영어발음을 향상시키는 방법

TONGUE TWISTER : 주의점은 cook과 good의 발음 차이

How many cookies could a good cook cook

If a good cook could cook cookies?

A good cook could cook as much cookies as a good cook

Who could cook cookies.

Topic 07

LEVEL 3

FISH THAT BREAK WIND

방귀 뀌는 물고기

Step ❶

Understanding

음원을 들으면서 눈으로 읽어 보고,
문제를 통해서 이해했는지 확인해 보세요.

Researchers have recently found that some fish do indeed "break wind." Scientists observed herring break wind, and they believe it is probably one of the means of exchanging information with each other. Researchers came to this conclusion for three reasons. First, when more herring were in a tank, they broke wind more often. Second, the herring were only causing a disturbance after dark. The sounds might help the fish find one another when they couldn't be seen. Third, researchers found out that herring can hear sounds at the breaking-wind frequency. Most other fish cannot hear sound at that frequency. That means that potential enemies didn't know that the herrings were communicating with each other.

 윗글의 밑줄 친 causing a disturbance가 의미하는 것은?

ⓐ bother
ⓑ make fun of
ⓒ make angry
ⓓ break wind

- break wind 방귀 뀌다, 트림하다
- herring 청어
- tank 수조

Step ❷

Listening

이번에는 억양과 끊어 읽기, 연음과 강조어에 대한 강의를 들어 보세요.

/ 끊어 읽기   ∫↘ 억양   **볼드색 강세를 두어 읽는 부분**   ‿ 연음

Researchers have recently found that some fish / **do** indeed "break wind."

Scientists observed herring break wind, / and they believe ∫ it is probably one of‿the means of / exchanging information with each other.

Researchers came to this ↘ conclusion for‿three reasons.

First, / when more herrings were in‿a tank, / they broke wind more often.

Second, / the herring were **only** causing a disturbance ∫ after dark. The sounds / might help the fish find one another / when‿they couldn't be‿seen.

Third, / researchers found out that / herring ∫ can hear sounds at‿the breaking-wind frequency.

Most other fish cannot ↘ hear sound / at that frequency.

That means ∫ that / potential enemies didn't know that‿the herrings were **communicating** with each other.

Step ❸

Read Slowly

스스로 끊어 읽기와 억양을 직접 표시하면서,
천천히 큰 소리로 읽어 보세요.

1회 ☐ 2회 ☐ 3회 ☐ 4회 ☐ 5회 ☐ 6회 ☐ 7회 ☐

Researchers have recently found that some fish do indeed "break wind."

Scientists observed herring break wind, and they believe it is probably one of the means of exchanging information with each other.

Researchers came to this conclusion for three reasons.

First, when more herring were in a tank, they broke wind more often.

Second, the herrings were only causing a disturbance after dark.

The sounds might help the fish find one another when they couldn't be seen.

Third, researchers found out that herring can hear sounds at the breaking-wind frequency.

Most other fish cannot hear sound at that frequency.

That means that potential enemies didn't know that the herrings were communicating with each other.

Step ④

Read Normal Speed with shadowing

자신이 생겼다면 이제 내용을 전달하면서 큰 소리로 따라 읽어 보세요.

1회 □   2회 □   3회 □   4회 □   5회 □   6회 □   7회 □

Step ⑤

Speak / Presentation

이제는 아래 글을 완성하면서 큰 소리로 사람들 앞에서 발표해 보세요.

Researchers have recently _____ _____ _____ fish do indeed "break wind." _____ _____ herring break wind, and they believe it is probably one of the means of exchanging information with each other. Researchers came to this conclusion _____ _____ _____. First, when more herring _____ ___ ___ _____, they broke wind more often. Second, the herring were only causing ___ _____ after dark. _____ _____ _____ help the fish find one another when they couldn't be seen. Third, researchers found out that herring can _____ _____ ___ ___ breaking-wind frequency. _____ _____ _____ cannot hear sound at that frequency. That means _____ _____ _____ didn't know that the herrings were communicating with each other.

◦ Script

최근 연구자들은 어떤 물고기들은 실제로 "방귀를 뀐다"는 사실을 알아냈다. 과학자들은 청어가 방귀를 뀌는 것을 관찰하고, 아마도 서로 정보를 교환하기 위한 수단의 일종으로 방귀를 뀌는 것으로 보고 있다. 과학자들은 세 가지 이유로 이 결론에 도달했다. 첫 번째 이유는 수조 안에 청어가 많을수록 더 자주 방귀를 뀐다는 사실이다. 두 번째로는 청어들은 어두워져서야 방귀를 뀐다는 것이다. 볼 수 없을 때 방귀 소리로 서로를 찾을 수 있게 돕는 것으로 보인다. 세 번째로, 과학자들은 청어가 방귀의 주파수 소리를 들을 수 있다는 것을 발견했다. 대부분의 다른 물고기들은 그 주파수의 소리를 들을 수 없다. 이는 청어의 잠재적인 적이 청어가 서로 의사소통을 하고 있는 것을 알 수 없다는 것을 의미한다.

● 정답 > d. break wind

Take a break

▶ 영어발음을 향상시키는 방법

TONGUE TWISTER : 주의점은 -ound 와 -og의 발음

How much ground would a groundhog hog,

If a groundhog could hog ground?

A groundhog would hog all the ground he could hog,

If a groundhog could hog ground.

Topic 08

LEVEL 3

THE COLORFUL RAINBOW

화려한 무지개

Step ❶

Understanding

음원을 들으면서 눈으로 읽어 보고,
문제를 통해서 이해했는지 확인해 보세요.

Most people believe that there are seven colors to every rainbow. Most picture books draw rainbows with red, indigo, violet, orange, yellow, green and blue lines. But in reality, there are actually a very large number of distinct colors in every rainbow. In between yellow and green, for example, you can find yellow-green, and greenish yellow-green, and so on and so forth. So, how many colors are there in a rainbow? It's not easy to say. It depends on the person looking at the rainbow as much as on the rainbow itself. Different people have a different ability to perceive different colors, while rainbows change slightly depending on several factors, like moisture, sunlight and time of day.

 윗글의 내용과 일치하지 않는 것은?

ⓐ There are not just seven colors in a rainbow.

ⓑ You can say exactly how many colors there are in a rainbow.

ⓒ You can find yellow-green, greenish yellow-green colors in a rainbow.

ⓓ People generally believe that there are seven colors in a rainbow.

  • indigo 남색   • moisture 습기

Step ❷

Listening

이번에는 억양과 끊어 읽기, 연음과 강조어에 대한
강의를 들어 보세요.

/ 끊어 읽기   ∫↘ 억양   볼드색 강세를 두어 읽는 부분   ‿ 연음

Most people believe that ↘there are seven colors / to **every** rainbow.

Most picture books draw rainbows with red, / indigo, / violet, / orange, / yellow, / green and blue lines.

But in reality, / there are actually / a very ∫large number‿of distinct colors ↘in **every** rainbow.

In between yellow and green, / for example, / you can find ↘ yellow-green, / and greenish yellow-green, / and so‿on and so‿forth.

So, / how ∫many colors are there ∫in‿a rainbow? ↘
It's not easy to say.

It depends on‿the person looking at the rainbow / as‿much as / on the **rainbow** itself.

Different people have‿a different ability ↘to perceive different colors, / while rainbows change **slightly** / depending on several factors, / like moisture, /sunlight and time‿of day.

Step ❸

Read Slowly

스스로 끊어 읽기와 억양을 직접 표시하면서,
천천히 큰 소리로 읽어 보세요.

1회 ☐ 2회 ☐ 3회 ☐ 4회 ☐ 5회 ☐ 6회 ☐ 7회 ☐

Most people believe that there are seven colors to every rainbow.

Most picture books draw rainbows with red, indigo, violet, orange, yellow, green and blue lines.

But in reality, there are actually a very large number of distinct colors in every rainbow.

In between yellow and green, for example, you can find yellow-green, and greenish yellow-green, and so on and so forth.

So, how many colors are there in a rainbow?

It's not easy to say.

It depends on the person looking at the rainbow as much as on the rainbow itself.

Different people have a different ability to perceive different colors, while rainbows change slightly depending on several factors, like moisture, sunlight and time of day.

Step ④

Read Normal Speed with shadowing
자신이 생겼다면 이제 내용을 전달하면서 큰 소리로 따라 읽어 보세요.

1회 ☐   2회 ☐   3회 ☐   4회 ☐   5회 ☐   6회 ☐   7회 ☐

Step ⑤

Speak / Presentation
이제는 아래 글을 완성하면서 큰 소리로 사람들 앞에서 발표해 보세요.

Most people believe that there are seven colors ___ ___ ___. Most picture books draw rainbows with red, indigo, violet, orange, yellow, ___ ___ ___ lines. But in reality, there are ___ ___ ___ ___ number of distinct colors in every rainbow. ___ ___ ___ and green, for example, you can find yellow-green, and greenish yellow-green, and so on and so forth. So, how many ___ ___ ___ in a rainbow? It's not ___ ___ ___. It depends on the person looking at the ___ ___ ___ ___ on the rainbow itself. Different people have a different ability ___ ___ different colors, while rainbows change slightly depending on several factors, like moisture, sunlight and time of day.

○ Script

대부분의 사람들은 무지개는 일곱 가지 색으로 되어 있다고 생각한다. 대부분의 그림책에서도 무지개를 빨간색, 남색, 보라색, 주황색, 노란색, 초록색, 파란색 선으로 그리고 있다. 하지만 실제로 모든 무지개는 각각 아주 많은 별개의 색으로 이루어져 있다. 예를 들어 노란색과 초록색만 봐도, 그 사이에 녹황색, 푸르스름한 녹황색 등이 있다. 그렇다면 무지개에는 몇 가지 색이 있을까? 단정을 짓기가 힘든 것은 무지개 색이 무지개 자체만큼이나 무지개를 보는 사람의 시각에 달려 있기 때문이다. 개개의 사람들은 각각 색을 지각하는 능력이 다르고, 무지개 역시 습기와 햇살, 그리고 시각과 같은 여러 요인에 의해 조금씩 변화한다.

● 정답 > b. You can say exactly how many colors there are in a rainbow.

Take a break

▶ 영어발음을 향상시키는 방법

TONGUE TWISTER : 주의점은 ch-와 -oo-의 발음

How much wood could Chuck Woods' woodchuck chuck, if Chuck Woods' woodchuck could and would chuck wood? If Chuck Woods' woodchuck could and would chuck wood, how much wood could and would Chuck Woods' woodchuck chuck? Chuck Woods' woodchuck would chuck, he would, as much as he could, and chuck as much wood as any woodchuck would, if a woodchuck could and would chuck wood.

Topic 09   LEVEL 3

THE BLUE SKY

파란 하늘

Step ❶

Understanding

음원을 들으면서 눈으로 읽어 보고,
문제를 통해서 이해했는지 확인해 보세요.

It is a common myth that the sky is blue because of a reflection of the seas and oceans. But, it is not true at all. In fact, blue light from the sun spreads around much more than all the other colors from the sun. That's what causes the sky to appear blue. Light is made up of electromagnetic waves, and the distance between two crests in this wave is called the wavelength. Red light, for instance, has the longest wavelength. The wavelength of blue light is about half that of red light. This difference in wavelength causes blue light to be scattered nearly ten times more than red light. Lord Rayleigh studied this phenomenon in detail, and that's why it is commonly called as "Rayleigh scattering." There are some scientists, however, who call this the Tyndall effect.

 윗글의 내용과 일치하는 것은?

ⓐ Light is made up of wavelengths.
ⓑ Red light spreads much more than all the other colors.
ⓒ Red light scatters nearly ten times more than blue light.
ⓓ The blue wavelength is about half that of red light.

- scattering 산란   - phenomenon 현상   - wavelength 파장
- electromagnetic wave 전자파

Step ❷

Listening

이번에는 억양과 끊어 읽기, 연음과 강조어에 대한 강의를 들어 보세요.

/ 끊어 읽기 ↗↘ 억양   볼드색 강세를 두어 읽는 부분   ‿ 연음

It is a common myth that / the sky is‿blue because of‿a reflection ↗ of the seas and oceans.
But, / it is not true at‿all.
In fact, / blue ↗ light from the sun ↘ spreads around **much more** / than all‿the other colors from the ↘ sun.
That's ↗ what causes the‿sky to appear blue.
Light is made up of electromagnetic waves, / and the distance between two crests in this wave / is called ↘ the wavelength.
Red light, / for instance, / has the **longest** wavelength.
The wavelength of blue light is about / half that of ↘ red light.
This difference in wavelength / causes blue light to‿be scattered / **nearly** ten times more ↗ than red light.
Lord Rayleigh studied this phenomenon in detail, / and that's why it‿is commonly called / as "Rayleigh scattering."
There are some scientists, / however, / who call this ↘ the Tyndall effect.

Step ❸

Read Slowly

스스로 끊어 읽기와 억양을 직접 표시하면서,
천천히 큰 소리로 읽어 보세요.

1회 ☐ 2회 ☐ 3회 ☐ 4회 ☐ 5회 ☐ 6회 ☐ 7회 ☐

It is a common myth that the sky is blue because of a reflection of the seas and oceans.

But, it is not true at all.

In fact, blue light from the sun spreads around much more than all the other colors from the sun.

That's what causes the sky to appear blue.

Light is made up of electromagnetic waves, and the distance between two crests in this wave is called the wavelength.

Red light, for instance, has the longest wavelength.

The wavelength of blue light is about half that of red light.

This difference in wavelength causes blue light to be scattered nearly ten times more than red light.

Lord Rayleigh studied this phenomenon in detail, and that's why it is commonly called as "Rayleigh scattering."

There are some scientists, however, who call this the Tyndall effect.

Step ④

Read Normal Speed with shadowing
자신이 생겼다면 이제 내용을 전달하면서 큰 소리로 따라 읽어 보세요.

1회 □ 2회 □ 3회 □ 4회 □ 5회 □ 6회 □ 7회 □

Step ⑤

Speak / Presentation
이제는 아래 글을 완성하면서 큰 소리로 사람들 앞에서 발표해 보세요.

It is ___ _____ ___ that the sky is blue because of a reflection of the seas and oceans. But, ___ ___ ___ ___ at all. In fact, blue light from the sun _____ _____ much more than all the other colors from the sun. That's what causes the sky to appear blue. Light ___ _____ ___ ___ electromagnetic waves, and the distance _____ ___ _____ in this wave is called the wavelength. Red light, for instance, has the longest wavelength. The wavelength of blue light ___ _____ _____ _____ of red light. ___ _____ ___ wavelength causes blue light to be scattered nearly ten times more than red light. Lord Rayleigh studied ____ _____ ___ _____, and _____ _____ it is commonly called as "Rayleigh scattering." There are some scientists, however, who call this the Tyndall effect.

○ Script

하늘은 바다와 대양이 반사되어 푸르다라는 것이 일반적인 통념이다. 그러나 그것은 전혀 사실이 아니다. 사실, 태양에서 온 푸른 광선은 다른 색의 광선들에 비해 훨씬 더 넓게 퍼진다. 그것이 하늘이 푸르게 보이는 이유이다. 빛은 전자파로 이루어져 있고, 파와 파 사이의 거리를 파장이라고 부른다. 예를 들어, 붉은 광선은 가장 긴 파장을 가지고 있다. 푸른 광선의 파장은 붉은 광선의 절반 정도의 길이이다. 이 파장의 차이로 인해 푸른 광선이 붉은 광선에 비해 거의 10배 이상 흩어진다. 레일리 경이 이 현상을 상세히 연구했는데, 그 때문에 이 현상은 '레일리 산란'이라고 불린다. 그러나 어떤 과학자들은 이 현상을 '틴들 효과'라고 부른다.

● 정답 > d. The blue wavelength is about half that of red light.

Take a break

▶ 영어발음을 향상시키는 방법

TONGUE TWISTER : 주의점은 -y의 발음

Why do you cry, Willy?

Why do you cry?

Why, Willy?

Why, Willy?

Why, Willy?

Why?

Topic 10

LEVEL 3

THE IMPORTANCE OF WATER

물의 중요성

Step ❶

Understanding

음원을 들으면서 눈으로 읽어 보고,
문제를 통해서 이해했는지 확인해 보세요.

Have you ever wondered how long you could live without water? You might be surprised to know just how important it really is! Before you were born, when you were in your mom's womb, your body contained 97% water. That figure fell to 77% when you were an infant. It fell to 60% when you became an adult. It will fall to less than 50% when you become an older person, too. You will experience pain and severe thirst if you lose as little as 1~2% of your body's water. With a 15% loss of water, your life will be threatened. You might survive for thirty days without food, but not without water. In less than a week, you will die if you have no water to drink. Yes, water certainly is important to your body!

 윗글의 제목으로 가장 알맞은 것은?
ⓐ The characteristics of water
ⓑ The damage from the loss of water
ⓒ The new way to use water
ⓓ The importance of water to our body

Voca.　• thirst 목마름, 갈증　• threaten 위협하다, 우려가 있다

Step ❷

Listening

이번에는 억양과 끊어 읽기, 연음과 강조어에 대한
강의를 들어 보세요.

/ 끊어 읽기   ↗↘ 억양   **볼드색** 강세를 두어 읽는 부분   ‿ 연음

Have you ever ↗ wondered how long you could live without water? ↗
You might be surprised to know ↘ just **how** important it **really** is!
Before you were born, / when you were in‿your mom's womb, / your body ↗ contained 97% water.
That figure fell to ↘ 77% when you‿were an infant.
It fell to ↘ 60% when you became an adult.
It will fall to less than 50% / when you become ↘ an older person, / too.
You ↗ will experience pain and severe thirst / if you lose **as** little as 1~2% of your body's ↘ water.
With a 15% loss of water, / your life will‿be threatened.
You might survive ↗ for thirty days without food, / but not ↘ without water.
In less than a week, / you will **die** if you have **no** water to drink.
Yes, / water certainly ↗ is important to‿your body!

Step ❸

Read Slowly

스스로 끊어 읽기와 억양을 직접 표시하면서,
천천히 큰 소리로 읽어 보세요.

1회 ☐   2회 ☐   3회 ☐   4회 ☐   5회 ☐   6회 ☐   7회 ☐

Have you ever wondered how long you could live without water?

You might be surprised to know just how important it really is!

Before you were born, when you were in your mom's womb, your body contained 97% water.

That figure fell to 77% when you were an infant.

It fell to 60% when you became an adult.

It will fall to less than 50% when you become an older person, too.

You will experience pain and severe thirst if you lose as little as 1~2% of your body's water.

With a 15% loss of water, your life will be threatened.

You might survive for thirty days without food, but not without water.

In less than a week, you will die if you have no water to drink.

Yes, water certainly is important to your body!

Step ❹ MP3

Read Normal Speed with shadowing

자신이 생겼다면 이제 내용을 전달하면서 큰 소리로 따라 읽어 보세요.

1회 □   2회 □   3회 □   4회 □   5회 □   6회 □   7회 □

Step ❺

Speak / Presentation

이제는 아래 글을 완성하면서 큰 소리로 사람들 앞에서 발표해 보세요.

Have you ever wondered how long you could live _____ _____? You might be surprised to know just _____ _____ _____ _____ is! _____ _____ _____ _____, when you were in your mom's womb, your body contained 97% water. That figure fell to 77% when _____ _____ _____ _____. It fell to 60% when you became _____ _____. It will fall to less than 50% _____ _____ _____ an older person, too. You will _____ _____ and severe thirst if you lose as little as 1~2% of your body's water. With a 15% loss of water, your life _____ _____ _____. You might survive for thirty days without food, _____ _____ _____ water. In less than a week, you will die _____ _____ _____ _____ water to drink. Yes, water _____ _____ important to your body!

○ Script

물을 마시지 않고 얼마나 살 수 있는지 궁금해 한 적이 있는가? 이것이 얼마나 중요한 것인지 알게 되면 놀랄지도 모른다! 이 세상에 태어나기 전에, 즉 어머니의 자궁에 있을 때는 신체의 97%가 물로 되어 있었다. 유아가 되면 그 수치는 77%로 떨어졌다가 성인이 되어서는 60%로 떨어지고, 나이를 더 먹으면 이 수치는 또 떨어져 50% 미만이 될 것이다. 신체에 있는 수분의 1~2%만 잃게 되어도 고통과 극심한 갈증을 느끼게 될 것이다. 15%를 잃으면 생명에 위협을 받는다. 음식을 먹지 않고는 30일 정도 살 수 있지만, 물을 마시지 않고는 그렇게 버틸 수 없다. 마실 물이 없으면 일주일 이내에 죽게 될 것이다. 그렇다, 물은 신체에 극히 중요한 것이다!

● 정답 > d. The importance of water to our body

Take a break

▶ 영어발음을 향상시키는 방법

TONGUE TWISTER : 주의점은 oa-와 -vy의 발음

Mares eat oats and does eat oats,

And little lambs eat ivy.

A Kid will eat ivy too, wouldn't you?

Topic 11 LEVEL 3

NATURAL FOODS PREVENT US FROM GETTING SICK

자연식품이 질병을 예방한다

Step ❶

Understanding

음원을 들으면서 눈으로 읽어 보고,
문제를 통해서 이해했는지 확인해 보세요.

Many foreigners think that no Korean suffered from SARS because we eat garlic. This is an example that shows food can be a natural pharmacy. Many food scientists and nutritionists believe that the solutions to many of our health problems can be found inside our everyday food. Scientists are still in the early age of understanding how the nutrients in natural food can help people to keep good health. However, they have discovered many things in individual foods that seem to help us keep away from certain diseases. For example, tea and broccoli prevent cancer while celery and oats help to lower blood pressure. There are many other natural foods that have been proven to prevent diseases.

Q! 윗글의 요지로 가장 알맞은 것은?
ⓐ There are lots of healthy food in Korea.
ⓑ Our daily food can be a natural pharmacy.
ⓒ Eating garlic is a good way to cure some diseases.
ⓓ Koreans didn't suffer from SARS because of garlic.

- garlic 마늘　・natural pharmacy 자연적인 약
- prevent 막다, 방지하다

Step ❷

Listening

이번에는 억양과 끊어 읽기, 연음과 강조어에 대한 강의를 들어 보세요.

/ 끊어 읽기   ∫ ↘ 억양   볼드색 강세를 두어 읽는 부분   ⌣ 연음

Many foreigners think that ↘ no Korean suffered from SARS / because we eat garlic.

This is an example that shows / food can be a natural pharmacy.

Many food scientists and nutritionists ∫ believe that / the solutions to many of our health problems / can be found inside our everyday food.

Scientists ∫ are still in the early age of understanding / how the nutrients in natural food / can help people to keep good health.

However, / they have discovered many things in individual foods ↘ that seem to help us keep away from ↘ certain diseases.

For example, / tea and broccoli prevent cancer / while celery and oats ∫ help to lower blood pressure.

There are many other natural foods / that have been **proven** to prevent diseases.

Step ❸

Read Slowly

스스로 끊어 읽기와 억양을 직접 표시하면서,
천천히 큰 소리로 읽어 보세요.

1회 □ 2회 □ 3회 □ 4회 □ 5회 □ 6회 □ 7회 □

Many foreigners think that no Korean suffered from SARS because we eat garlic.

This is an example that shows food can be a natural pharmacy.

Many food scientists and nutritionists believe that the solutions to many of our health problems can be found inside our everyday food.

Scientists are still in the early age of understanding how the nutrients in natural food can help people to keep good health.

However, they have discovered many things in individual foods that seem to help us keep away from certain diseases.

For example, tea and broccoli prevent cancer while celery and oats help to lower blood pressure.

There are many other natural foods that have been proven to prevent diseases.

Step ④

Read Normal Speed with shadowing
자신이 생겼다면 이제 내용을 전달하면서 큰 소리로 따라 읽어 보세요.

1회 ☐   2회 ☐   3회 ☐   4회 ☐   5회 ☐   6회 ☐   7회 ☐

Step ⑤

Speak / Presentation
이제는 아래 글을 완성하면서 큰 소리로 사람들 앞에서 발표해 보세요.

_____ _____ _____ that no Korean suffered from SARS because we eat garlic. This is an example that shows food can be a _____ _____. Many food _____ ___ _____ believe that the solutions to many of our health problems can be found inside our everyday food. Scientists are still ____ _____ _____ _____ ____ understanding how the nutrients in natural food can help people to keep good health. However, they have discovered many things in individual foods that seem to help ____ _____ _____ ____ certain diseases. For example, tea and broccoli prevent cancer _____ _____ ____ _____ help to lower blood pressure. There are many other _____ _____ ____ have been proven to prevent diseases.

○ Script

마늘을 먹기 때문에 한국인들은 SARS에 걸리지 않았다고 생각하는 외국인들이 많다. 이것은 음식이 자연적인 약이 될 수 있다는 것을 보여 주는 하나의 예이다. 우리의 건강에 관련된 문제 중 상당 부분은 일상적인 음식 안에서 그 해결책을 찾을 수 있다고 믿는 식품 과학자들과 영양학자들이 많다. 자연식품에 들어 있는 영양소가 사람들의 건강 유지에 어떤 도움이 되는지에 대해 과학자들은 아직 이해의 초기 단계에 있다. 그러나 과학자들은 개개의 식품에서 어떤 것들은 우리가 어떤 질병을 멀리하는 데 도움을 준다는 것을 발견했다. 예를 들면, 홍차와 브로콜리는 암을 예방하고, 샐러리와 귀리는 혈압을 낮추는 데 도움이 된다. 그 외에도 우리의 질병을 막는 것으로 증명된 자연식품이 많이 있다.

● 정답 > b. Our daily food can be a natural pharmacy.

Take a break

▶ 영어발음을 향상시키는 방법

TONGUE TWISTER : 주의점은 -aw의 발음

As I was in Arkansas I saw a saw

That could out saw any saw I ever saw saw.

If you happen to be in Arkansas and see a saw that can out saw the saw I saw saw I'd like to see the saw you saw saw.

Topic 12

LEVEL 3

ALFRED NOBEL

알프레드 노벨

Step ❶

Understanding

음원을 들으면서 눈으로 읽어 보고,
문제를 통해서 이해했는지 확인해 보세요.

Alfred Nobel was born on October 21st in 1833. He was the person who made dynamite. Many people around the world wanted to buy dynamite so Alfred became very rich quickly. He was very proud of himself and his invention at first, because he thought his invention will contribute to human beings welfare and development. Sadly, contrary to his expectation, one of the greatest inventions in history played its role as an extremely deadly weapon. People used dynamite for not only doing good for human beings but also for killing each other. Due to this, Alfred Nobel decided to give most of his money away to other people before his death. He started the Nobel Prize and some of his money is given away every October to the winners.

 윗글의 주제로 알맞은 것은?
ⓐ The origin of dynamite
ⓑ Alfred Nobel's life
ⓒ The importance of Nobel Prize
ⓓ The history of Nobel Peace Prize

- contribute 기여하다, 공헌하다
- welfare 복지

Step ❷

Listening

이번에는 억양과 끊어 읽기, 연음과 강조어에 대한
강의를 들어 보세요.

/ 끊어 읽기　↗↘ 억양　**볼드색** 강세를 두어 읽는 부분　⌣ 연음

Alfred Nobel ↘ was born ⌣ on October 21st in 1833.
He was ⌣ the person who made dynamite.
Many people around the world / wanted to buy dynamite / so Alfred ↗ became **very** rich quickly.
He was very proud of himself and ⌣ his invention at first, / because he thought his invention will contribute ↗ to human beings welfare and development.
Sadly, / contrary to his expectation, / one of ⌣ the greatest inventions in history ↘ played its role as ⌣ an **extremely** deadly weapon.
People used dynamite for not only doing good for human beings / but **also** for killing each other.
Due to this, / Alfred Nobel decided to give most of his money away ↘ to other people / before his death.
He started the Nobel Prize / and some of ⌣ his money is given away **every** October to the ↗ winners.

Step ❸

Read Slowly

스스로 끊어 읽기와 억양을 직접 표시하면서,
천천히 큰 소리로 읽어 보세요.

1회 ☐ 2회 ☐ 3회 ☐ 4회 ☐ 5회 ☐ 6회 ☐ 7회 ☐

Alfred Nobel was born on October 21st in 1833.

He was the person who made dynamite.

Many people around the world wanted to buy dynamite so Alfred became very rich quickly.

He was very proud of himself and his invention at first, because he thought his invention will contribute to human beings welfare and development.

Sadly, contrary to his expectation, one of the greatest inventions in history played its role as an extremely deadly weapon.

People used dynamite for not only doing good for human beings but also for killing each other.

Due to this, Alfred Nobel decided to give most of his money away to other people before his death.

He started the Nobel Prize and some of his money is given away every October to the winners.

Step ❹   MP3

Read Normal Speed with shadowing

자신이 생겼다면 이제 내용을 전달하면서 큰 소리로 따라 읽어 보세요.

1회 □   2회 □   3회 □   4회 □   5회 □   6회 □   7회 □

Step ❺

Speak / Presentation

이제는 아래 글을 완성하면서 큰 소리로 사람들 앞에서 발표해 보세요.

Alfred Nobel was _____ ____ October 21st in 1833. He was ____ _____ ____ made dynamite. Many people around the world wanted ___ ___ _____ so Alfred became very rich quickly. He was very proud of himself and _____ _____ ___ _____, because he thought his invention will contribute to human beings welfare and development. Sadly, _____ ____ _____ expectation, one of the greatest inventions in history played its role as an extremely deadly weapon. People _____ _____ ____ not only doing good for human beings but also for killing each other. Due to this, Alfred Nobel decided to give _____ ___ ___ _____ away to other people before his death. He started the Nobel Prize and some of his money is _____ _____ _____ October to the winners.

○ Script

알프레드 노벨은 1833년 10월 21일에 태어났다. 이 사람이 다이너마이트를 발명했다. 전 세계적으로 다이너마이트를 사고 싶어 하는 사람들이 많았기 때문에 알프레드는 금방 큰 부자가 되었다. 처음에 알프레드는 자신과 자신의 발명품에 대해서 아주 자랑스러워했다. 왜냐하면, 자신이 발명한 다이너마이트가 인류의 복지와 개발에 기여할 것이라고 생각했기 때문이다. 슬프게도, 알프레드의 기대와는 반대로 인류 역사상 가장 위대한 발명품에 속하는 이것은 아주 치명적인 무기의 역할을 하게 되었다. 사람들은 다이너마이트를 인류를 위해서 좋은 일로만 사용한 것이 아니라, 서로 죽이는 데도 사용했다. 이로 인해 알프레드 노벨은 죽기 전에 자신의 돈 대부분을 다른 사람에게 주기로 했다. 그는 노벨상을 만들었고 지금도 매년 10월에 수상자들은 노벨의 돈의 일부를 받게 된다.

- **정답** > b. Alfred Nobel's life

Take a break

▶ 영어발음을 향상시키는 방법

TONGUE TWISTER : 주의점은 be-와 ba-의 발음

How many berries could a bare berry carry,

If a bare berry could carry berries?

Well they can't carry berries

(Which could make you very wary)

But a bare berry carried is more scary!

Topic 13 LEVEL 3

THE BRIDAL SHOWER

신부 파티

Step ❶

Understanding

음원을 들으면서 눈으로 읽어 보고,
문제를 통해서 이해했는지 확인해 보세요.

Have you ever been invited to a bridal shower? When a woman gets married in America, she usually has a bridal shower a few weeks before the wedding. A bridal or wedding shower is a party to celebrate a woman's future marriage to a man. The event is called a shower because the bride's family and friends want to shower her with gifts and good wishes. Some brides have more than one shower because several friends and family members host showers for her. Bridal shower guests often enjoy good food, traditional and non-traditional bridal shower games, giving advice for a good marriage, and watching the bride open gifts.

 윗글의 제목으로 가장 알맞은 것은?
ⓐ Bride and groom
ⓑ A bridal shower
ⓒ The way of enjoying shower
ⓓ Wedding ceremony

- bridal shower 신부 파티

Step ❷

Listening

이번에는 억양과 끊어 읽기, 연음과 강조어에 대한
강의를 들어 보세요.

/ 끊어 읽기   ↗↘ 억양   **볼드색** 강세를 두어 읽는 부분   ‿ 연음

Have you ↗ ever been invited to a bridal shower? ↗
When a woman gets married in America, / she usually has‿a bridal shower / a few weeks before the wedding.
A bridal or wedding shower ↘ is a party / to celebrate a woman's future marriage to a man.
The event ↗ is called a shower / because the bride's family and friends want‿to shower her / with gifts ↗ and good wishes.
Some brides have more than one ↘ shower / because several friends and family members host showers for‿her.
Bridal shower guests **often** enjoy good food, / traditional and ↘ non-traditional bridal shower games, / giving advice for a good marriage, / and ↗ watching the‿bride open gifts.

Step ❸

Read Slowly

스스로 끊어 읽기와 억양을 직접 표시하면서,
천천히 큰 소리로 읽어 보세요.

1회 ☐ 2회 ☐ 3회 ☐ 4회 ☐ 5회 ☐ 6회 ☐ 7회 ☐

Have you ever been invited to a bridal shower?

When a woman gets married in America, she usually has a bridal shower a few weeks before the wedding.

A bridal or wedding shower is a party to celebrate a woman's future marriage to a man.

The event is called a shower because the bride's family and friends want to shower her with gifts and good wishes.

Some brides have more than one shower because several friends and family members host showers for her.

Bridal shower guests often enjoy good food, traditional and non-traditional bridal shower games, giving advice for a good marriage, and watching the bride open gifts.

Step ④

Read Normal Speed with shadowing

자신이 생겼다면 이제 내용을 전달하면서 큰 소리로 따라 읽어 보세요.

1회 ☐ 2회 ☐ 3회 ☐ 4회 ☐ 5회 ☐ 6회 ☐ 7회 ☐

Step ⑤

Speak / Presentation

이제는 아래 글을 완성하면서 큰 소리로 사람들 앞에서 발표해 보세요.

Have you ever been _____ ___ ___ bridal shower? _____ ___ _____ _____ married in America, she usually has a bridal shower a few weeks before the wedding. A bridal or wedding shower ____ ___ _____ ___ celebrate a woman's future marriage to a man. The event is called a shower because the bride's _____ _____ _____ want to shower her with gifts and good wishes. Some brides have more than one shower because several friends and family members _____ _____ for her. Bridal shower guests _____ _____ _____ food, traditional and non-traditional bridal shower games, giving advice for a good marriage, and watching the bride open gifts.

○ Script

신부 파티에 초대를 받은 적이 있는가? 미국에서는 여성이 결혼하게 되면, 결혼식이 열리기 몇 주 전에 보통 신부 파티를 열게 된다. 신부 파티 또는 결혼 파티란 남성과 앞으로 결혼하게 되는 여성을 축하해 주는 파티이다. 신부의 가족이나 친구들이 선물과 행복을 기원하는 인사를 소나기처럼 신부에게 "샤워"해 준다고 해서 이를 샤워라고 부른다. 어떤 신부는 여러 친구나 가족이 별도로 파티를 해 주기 때문에 이 행사를 여러 번 하는 경우도 있다. 신부 파티에 참석한 사람들은 맛있는 음식을 먹으며, 전통적이거나 비전통적인 파티 게임을 하기도 하고, 행복한 결혼 생활을 위한 조언을 하고, 신부가 선물 포장을 여는 것을 보기도 하면서 즐기는 경우가 많다.

● 정답 > b. A bridal shower

Take a break

▶ 영어발음을 향상시키는 방법

TONGUE TWISTER : 주의점은 can-의 발음

If you can't can any candy can,

How many candy cans can a candy canner can

If he can can candy cans?

Topic 14 LEVEL 3

GET AWAY FROM THE INDOOR AIR POLLUTANTS

실내 공기 오염물을 퇴치하자

Step ❶

Understanding
음원을 들으면서 눈으로 읽어 보고,
문제를 통해서 이해했는지 확인해 보세요.

Are you coughing, sneezing and having a headache all the time inside your house? Do you know that the air in our houses and buildings can be more polluted than the outdoor air? We spend most of our time indoors. So it's important to breathe clean indoor air to keep ourselves healthy. Many people, especially babies, children and seniors can easily get health problems by indoor air pollutants. Some of common indoor air pollutants are animal dander, indoor molds, cleaning products, tobacco smoke, and perfumes. What can you do? There are several things we can do in order to control air pollutants. We need to dust, clean frequently with a vacuum cleaner, use fan to dry the carpet, clean up food scraps promptly, cover trash containers, and have a professional service spray once in a while.

 윗글의 내용과 일치하지 않는 것은?

ⓐ You may have a headache because of the indoor air pollutants.
ⓑ Children can easily get sick by indoor air pollutants.
ⓒ Inside of your house can be dirtier than the outside.
ⓓ There's nothing that you can do to make indoor air clean.

- pollutant 오염물
- animal dander 동물의 비듬
- indoor molds 실내 곰팡이
- promptly 재빨리

Step ❷

Listening

이번에는 억양과 끊어 읽기, 연음과 강조어에 대한 강의를 들어 보세요.

/ 끊어 읽기   ∫↘ 억양   **볼드색** 강세를 두어 읽는 부분   ‿ 연음

Are you coughing, / sneezing and having a headache all the time inside your house? ∫

Do you know ∫ that the air in our houses and buildings / can be **more** polluted than the outdoor air? ∫

We spend most of‿our time indoors.

So it's important ∫ to breathe clean indoor air to‿keep ourselves healthy.

Many people, / especially babies, / children and seniors can **easily** get health problems ↘ by indoor air pollutants.

Some of common indoor air pollutants / are animal dander, / indoor molds, / cleaning products, / tobacco smoke, / and perfumes.

What ∫ can you do? ↘

There are **several** things ↘ we can do in‿order to control air pollutants.

We need to dust, / clean frequently with‿a vacuum cleaner, / use fan to dry the carpet, / clean up food scraps promptly, / cover trash containers, / and‿have a professional service spray once ↘ in a‿while.

Step ❸

Read Slowly

스스로 끊어 읽기와 억양을 직접 표시하면서,
천천히 큰 소리로 읽어 보세요.

1회 ☐ 2회 ☐ 3회 ☐ 4회 ☐ 5회 ☐ 6회 ☐ 7회 ☐

Are you coughing, sneezing and having a headache all the time inside your house?

Do you know that the air in our houses and buildings can be more polluted than the outdoor air?

We spend most of our time indoors.

So it's important to breathe clean indoor air to keep ourselves healthy.

Many people, especially babies, children and seniors can easily get health problems by indoor air pollutants.

Some of the common indoor air pollutants are animal dander, indoor molds, cleaning products, tobacco smoke, and perfumes.

What can you do?

There are several things we can do in order to control air pollutants.

We need to dust, clean frequently with a vacuum cleaner, use fan to dry the carpet, clean up food scraps promptly, cover trash containers, and have a professional service spray once in a while.

Step ④

Read Normal Speed with shadowing
자신이 생겼다면 이제 내용을 전달하면서 큰 소리로 따라 읽어 보세요.

1회 □   2회 □   3회 □   4회 □   5회 □   6회 □   7회 □

Step ⑤

Speak / Presentation
이제는 아래 글을 완성하면서 큰 소리로 사람들 앞에서 발표해 보세요.

Are you coughing, sneezing and having a headache ____ ____ ____ inside your house? Do you know that the air in our houses and buildings can be more _____ ____ ____ outdoor air? We spend most of our ____ _____. So it's important to breathe ____ _____ ____ to keep ourselves healthy. Many people, especially babies, children and seniors can easily get health _____ ____ ____ air pollutants. Some of common indoor air pollutants are animal dander, indoor molds, _____ _____, tobacco smoke, and perfumes. What can you do? There are several things we can do ____ _____ ____ _____ air pollutants. We need to dust, _____ _____ _____ a vacuum cleaner, use fan to dry the carpet, clean up food scraps promptly, cover trash containers, and have a professional service spray once in a while.

○ Script

집 안에 있으면 항상 기침과 재채기를 하고 머리가 아픈가? 집이나 건물 안의 공기가 바깥 공기보다 더 오염되어 있을 수 있다는 사실을 알고 있는가? 우리는 대부분의 시간을 실내에서 보낸다. 따라서 건강하게 지내려면 깨끗한 실내 공기를 마시는 것이 중요하다. 특히 아기들, 어린이들, 고령자를 비롯해 많은 사람들이 실내 공기 오염 물질 때문에 쉽게 건강상의 문제를 일으킨다. 실내 공기 오염 물질 중에서 흔한 것으로는, 동물의 피부에서 떨어진 비듬, 실내 곰팡이, 세제, 담배 연기, 향수를 들 수 있다. 그러면 어떻게 하면 될까? 실내 공기 오염 물질을 해결할 수 있는 방법에는 여러 가지가 있다. 자주 먼지를 털어 내고, 진공청소기로 청소를 하고, 선풍기를 사용해서 카펫을 말리고, 음식 부스러기를 빨리 치우고, 쓰레기통을 뚜껑으로 덮고, 가끔 전문적인 청소업자에게 맡겨서 실내에 소독약을 뿌린다.

● 정답 > d. There's nothing that you can do to make indoor air clean.

Take a break

▶ 영어발음을 향상시키는 방법

TONGUE TWISTER : 주의점은 dr- 와 -ew-의 발음

How much dew does a dewdrop drop

If dewdrops do drop dew?

They do drop, they do

As do dewdrops drop

If dewdrops do drop dew.

Topic 15

LEVEL 3

WHAT IS A PIGGY BANK?

돼지 저금통이란?

Step ❶

Understanding

음원을 들으면서 눈으로 읽어 보고,
문제를 통해서 이해했는지 확인해 보세요.

You may have one or two piggy banks in your house. Have you ever wondered how the piggy bank got its name? The story of the piggy bank starts with the word "pygg." Pygg was the name of a kind of clay found in England. People used to make many household ceramic objects from pygg. A book called *Extraordinary Origins of Everyday Things* by Charles Panati claims that people saved money in jars made with pygg in the kitchen. Somehow by the 18th century, a pygg jar had been transformed into the shape of a pig. Perhaps, it was because the word "pygg" was originally pronounced like pig.

 윗글에서 돼지 저금통이란 이름으로 불리게 된 결정적인 이유로 알맞은 것은?

ⓐ The popularity of a pig
ⓑ The meaning of the word pygg
ⓒ The belief that the word pygg has luck
ⓓ The similarity of pronunciation

Voca.
- piggy bank 돼지 저금통
- wonder 궁금해 하다
- extraordinary 놀라운

Step ❷

Listening

이번에는 억양과 끊어 읽기, 연음과 강조어에 대한
강의를 들어 보세요.

/ 끊어 읽기   ∫ ↘ 억양   **볼드색 강세를 두어 읽는 부분**   ‿ 연음

You may ↘ have one or two piggy banks in‿your house.
Have you ∫ ever wondered how the piggy bank got its name? ∫
The story of‿the piggy bank starts with the word "pygg."
Pygg / was the name of‿a kind of clay found in ↘England.
People used to make **many** household ceramic objects from pygg.
A book called / *Extraordinary Origins of Everyday Things* / by
Charles Panati / claims ∫ that people saved money in‿jars made
with pygg in the kitchen.
Somehow / by the 18th century, / a pygg ∫ jar had been
transformed into the ↘ shape of‿a pig.
Perhaps, / it was because the word pygg was originally
pronounced like / pig.

Step ❸

Read Slowly

스스로 끊어 읽기와 억양을 직접 표시하면서,
천천히 큰 소리로 읽어 보세요.

1회 ☐ 2회 ☐ 3회 ☐ 4회 ☐ 5회 ☐ 6회 ☐ 7회 ☐

You may have one or two piggy banks in your house.

Have you ever wondered how the piggy bank got its name?

The story of the piggy bank starts with the word "pygg."

Pygg was the name of a kind of clay found in England.

People used to make many household ceramic objects from pygg.

A book called *Extraordinary Origins of Everyday Things* by Charles Panati claims that people saved money in jars made with pygg in the kitchen.

Somehow by the 18th century, a pygg jar had been transformed into the shape of a pig.

Perhaps, it was because the word pygg was originally pronounced like pig.

Step ④

Read Normal Speed with shadowing

자신이 생겼다면 이제 내용을 전달하면서 큰 소리로 따라 읽어 보세요.

1회 □ 2회 □ 3회 □ 4회 □ 5회 □ 6회 □ 7회 □

Step ⑤

Speak / Presentation

이제는 아래 글을 완성하면서 큰 소리로 사람들 앞에서 발표해 보세요.

You may have one or two piggy banks ___ _____ _____.
Have you ____ _____ how the piggy bank got its name?
The story of the piggy bank _____ ___ _____ word "pygg."
Pygg was the name ___ __ _____ of clay found in England.
People used to make many household ceramic _____ _____
_____. A book called *Extraordinary Origins of Everyday Things* by Charles Panati _____ _____ people saved money in jars made with pygg in the kitchen. _____ ___ ___ 18th century, a pygg jar had been transformed into the shape of a pig. Perhaps, it was because the word pygg was _____ _____ like pig.

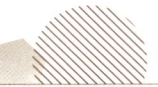

○ Script

집에 돼지 저금통 한두 개 정도는 가지고 있을 것이다. 그런데 돼지 저금통이란 이름이 어떻게 해서 생겼는지 궁금하게 생각해 본 적이 있는가? 돼지 저금통(piggy bank)에 관한 이야기는 "pygg"라는 말에서 시작된다. 이 피그라는 말은 잉글랜드 지역에서 출토되었던 진흙을 가리키던 것이었다. 사람들은 전에는 가정에서 사용하던 도기를 이 흙으로 빚었다. 찰스 퍼네티가 지은 "일상 용품의 놀라운 유래"라는 책에 의하면, 당시 사람들은 돈을 부엌 안에 피그로 만든 단지에 모아두었다고 한다. 그러다가 18세기가 될 무렵에는, 어쩐 일인지 이 피그로 만든 단지가 돼지 모양을 하게 되었다. 아마도 이 "pygg"라는 말이 원래는 "피그(pig)"처럼 발음되었기 때문인 모양이다.

● 정답 > d. The similarity of pronunciation

Take a break

▶ 영어발음을 향상시키는 방법

TONGUE TWISTER : 주의점은 fr- 와 -sh의 발음

Fresh fried fish,

Fish fresh fried,

Fried fish fresh,

Fish fried fresh.